"This book is a breath of fresh air, not because it's personal (which it is), or because it's practical (which it is), but because it is profoundly biblical. We found Gloria's Scripture-saturated counsel to be eminently realistic and deeply encouraging. Her wit and wisdom will be good for the pastor and good for the pastor's wife, which is good news for those in ministry and good news for the church."

Kevin and Trisha DeYoung, Senior Pastor, University Reformed Church, East Lansing, Michigan. Kevin and Trisha have been married for twelve years and have six children.

"Pastor's wives are deep in the trenches of gospel work. We need biblical truths that meet us there and help us joyfully persevere. Gloria Furman has given us a rich, gospel-saturated resource, drawing our eyes away from any prescribed role and setting them on the one who really does the work."

Christine Hoover, author, *The Church Planting Wife* and *From Good to Grace*

"Make no mistake: your role as a pastor's wife is essential. Gloria reminds us all to first and foremost drink deeply from the living water of Jesus as we endeavor to humbly fulfill our calling to love our husbands and the body of Christ to whom we have been called."

Jennifer Carter, wife of Matt Carter, Pastor of Preaching, Austin Stone Community Church, Austin, Texas

"Gloria Furman has given the church a much-needed gift by addressing a group that is often neglected—the wives of pastors. With the power of the gospel, the clarity of Scripture, and personal insight, Gloria helps pastor's wives to first draw near to Jesus as their greatest need and satisfaction, then to love and support their husbands, and finally to find a healthy place in the local church."

Joe and Jen Thorn, author, *Experiencing the Trinity* and *Note to Self*; Lead Pastor, Redeemer Fellowship, St. Charles, Illinois; and his wife, Jen, blogger, *jenthorn.com*

D1041567

"This book reminded me that when I'm weary, Christ's strength sustains me; when I'm tempted to cave in to expectations, I'm free to love and please Christ above all. Whether you're a pastor's wife or a military wife or a door sweeper's wife, this book will encourage you to plumb the riches of God's grace to you in Christ."

> **Kristie Anyabwile,** wife of Thabiti Anyabwile, Assistant Pastor for Church Planting, Capitol Hill Baptist Church, Washington, DC; mom of three; discipler of women

"Minister's wives lead unique lives with a unique set of challenges. Gloria does a beautiful job of reminding us that our identity is in Christ and his redemptive blood, not in the way we serve or how much we *do* for Christ. I felt encouraged and spurred on in my walk with the Lord to look upward to Christ and not at my outward circumstances. This is a very helpful book for minister's wives anywhere at any stage of life."

> **Heather Platt,** wife of David Platt, President, International Mission Board; author, *Radical*

"The pastor's wife bears unusual responsibility. Though the Bible is completely silent about her role, churches tend to load her with unfair and unrealistic expectation. Gloria Furman brings both sense and hope, showing from the Bible what God does and does not expect from her. And because she looks constantly to the Bible, this is a book that transcends both time and culture. I happily commend this book to pastors, their wives, and their churches."

> **Tim Challies,** author, *The Next Story*; blogger, *Challies.com*

"Gloria Furman gives practical and godly advice to those who are already serving as pastors' wives as well as those who are just starting out. Many pastors' wives feel the pressure to be someone they are not, wanting to be liked by everyone, or struggling with the juggle of family life and service. Gloria draws us to Scripture and back to our first love. *The Pastor's Wife* will help you avoid pitfalls and inspire you to stay close to Jesus and to find your strength in him. It reminded me of all I value about being a pastor's wife."

> **Carrie Vibert,** wife of Simon Vibert, Vice Principal and Director, The School of Preaching at Wycliffe Hall, Oxford

The Pastor's Wife

Other Crossway books by Gloria Furman

Glimpses of Grace: Treasuring the Gospel in Your Home (2013)

Treasuring Christ When Your Hands Are Full: Gospel Meditations for Busy Moms (2014)

GLORIA FURMAN

THE PASTOR'S WIFE

Strengthened by Grace for a Life of Love

::: CROSSWAY

WHEATON, ILLINOIS

Trade paperback ISBN: 978-1-4335-4383-8
ePub ISBN: 978-1-4335-4386-9
PDF ISBN: 978-1-4335-4384-5
Mobipocket ISBN: 978-1-4335-4385-2

Library of Congress Cataloging-in-Publication Data
Furman, Gloria, 1980–
The pastor's wife : strengthened by grace for a life of love / Gloria Furman.
  pages cm
 Includes bibliographical references and index.
 ISBN 978-1-4335-4383-8 (tp)
1. Spouses of clergy. 2. Wives—Religious life. I. Title.
BV4395.F87   2015
253'.22—dc23   2014037744

Crossway is a publishing ministry of Good News Publishers.

VP		25	24	23	22	21	20	19	18	17	16	15
15	14	13	12	11	10	9	8	7	6	5	4	3	2

Contents

Preface

You need to know that I am writing a book to ministry wives not from a position of having "been there, done that" after decades of faithful service. I'm not standing at the end of the road looking back. I am, rather, in the middle of it all. My husband and I were married three weeks after he started seminary, and we have been in full-time ministry together ever since. That was about thirteen years ago. So this is not a memoir in which I offer you my personal wisdom. That is my "dis-claimer." My "claimer," then, is what I do have and hope to share with you. Namely, I feel an acute sensibility of our need for God's grace to press on in ministry and a conviction that nothing but the blood of Jesus is all our hope and peace.

I'm finishing up this draft after two months of overwhelming ministry that's been riddled with valleys and peaks. We had our annual Easter sunrise service on the shore of the Arabian Gulf, and my heart soared as we watched the sun rise over our city. We sang about our risen and conquering Savior. In that sea we baptized ten people from five different countries, knowing that on the other side of that body of water we have brothers and sisters suffering and in prison because of their faith.

The next day I went to the grocery store where several of our friends work as cashiers. The women were distraught as they told me that my Nepalese friend Sumita had literally dropped dead in front of them the night before, seizing and vomiting blood. She was twenty years old and died apart from Christ. Shaken, I crossed the street with my groceries, and my preschool son repeatedly asked me, "Is Sumita with Jesus? Where is she?" Later that week it came to light that some false teaching has been threatening the faith of some of our church members, and the elders have spent many late nights talking and praying about what to do. The next week we discovered that a first-grade girl we know had been watching Internet pornography and was telling her classmates at school about what she had discovered. Then we received news that three doctors who had worshiped together with us on Good Friday had been shot and killed in a nearby country, martyred for their faith in Christ and for the good works they had done in his name. They had worshiped the Lamb by faith a week before, and now they see him face-to-face. The week that followed brought news that yet another friend from the grocery store had died suddenly, apart from Christ. Soon afterward my husband and I counseled a brokenhearted ministry couple who were suffering from the aftermath of her being raped and extorted for money. This type of counseling may seem like a once-in-a-ministry occasion to most, but, sadly, to some ministers it is common. The pervasiveness of our sin can even deeply wound those who are married to men in ministry.[1] Who is sufficient for these things (2 Cor. 2:16)?

You may read some humorous accounts in this book, but I assure you, I do not believe that ministry by the Word through the Spirit is a joke. What I aim to do here is help lift your gaze to see the supernatural nature in what we are doing as we serve alongside our husbands in ministry. We need courage, strength, faithfulness, humility, and joy. We need to see Christ as our sufficient Savior. We need childlike faith to serve in ministry alongside our husbands—faith that God is glad to give us. The life of Christ in us is our empowering, equipping, unleashing energy for personal holiness and service in God's kingdom. It is his strength that gives us what we need in order to nurture life in the face of death and through a million deaths-to-self each day. We need to remember that even the little blueberry-sized fruits produced by the Holy Spirit through Christ's people are part and parcel of his kingdom, where his will is done. Our anchor must be cast on Christ, and our foundation must be his Word, because there's no way we can love our Chief Shepherd, and the under-shepherd we are married to, and the bride we have been united to (Christ's people, the church) unless we have first seen how

Jesus loves us and gives us everything we need for life and godliness. We learn of Christ's love foremost in the sufficient, authoritative, understandable Word of God, and that's why the text of the Bible is our focus.

There's no way a finite heart can hold all the things we face in life and ministry, but Christ can, he does, and he will. Expectations of the minister's wife swirl all around us. The joy available to us is resplendent and everywhere. The needs press in on us from every side. The grief and horror we experience because of our sin is appalling and replete. Are you burdened not only by the needs of others in your church but by your own as well? I want to show you in this book that Jesus will carry those burdens too (Isa. 40:11; 41:10).

No matter how old you are or however long you've been married or served in ministry, I think we can all humbly agree that we have a need for endurance to live kingdom-oriented lives in this dark and fallen place (Heb. 10:36). The endurance we seek is no grim drudgery but a glad dependence on Jesus for a life of love strengthened by grace. That's what I hope you find in the pages of this little book.

Acknowledgments

Geometry is best done in community. Yes, geometry. But isn't this a book about the gospel, the church, and being married to a man who works in ministry? Certainly. Paul prayed that together "with all the saints," we would have strength to comprehend the breadth and length and height and depth of Christ's love (Eph. 3:17–18). We need each other in order to have the strength to stay focused on and dwell deeply in this kind of "geometry." I'm an undeserving recipient of the grace of such a community.

I'm thankful for the many ministry wives who helped me work through the content of this book. In these pages you'll notice the influence and wisdom particularly of these godly women: *Megan Hill*, *Melanie Yong*, *Bev Berrus*, and *Jen Thorn*. I'm grateful for your careful comments, discerning questions, and enthusiastic encouragement for this book. I pray that every ministry wife might know the strengthening love of Christian sisters like you!

Thank you, everyone at *Crossway*, for taking such great joy and care in publishing books for the good of the church.

Though I'll never know exactly how much work has gone into putting this resource together, I'm thankful for all the thousands of tasks that you did so cheerfully as unto the Lord. Special thanks go to *Justin Taylor, Lydia Brownback, Josh Dennis, Angie Cheatham, Amy Kruis, Matt Tully*, and *Janni Firestone*.

And on behalf of ministry wives everywhere (if I may be so bold)—to *the countless, unnamed ministry wives who suffer loss for the sake of the gospel*—thank you. We remember our sisters whose husbands are in prison, or are in prison themselves, as though we were in prison with you. We remember you who are mistreated, since we also are in the body. You have gone to Christ outside the camp and borne the reproach that he endured. Your faith reminds us that we have no lasting city here. And when we forget or flag in our zeal, your commitment to keep trusting in our unshakable God strengthens our resolve as well. By grace through faith we will share sweet fellowship together in the city that is to come.

And thank you to *my husband, Dave*, who shepherds others in the way of Christ by his strength and for his glory.

Introduction

"*There* you are," a woman whispered in my ear as she grabbed my elbow during a church gathering. "I've been looking *everywhere* for you!"

Startled, I braced myself. You never know what a statement like that could mean, especially at a church gathering. Did I leave the trunk of my car open (again)? Did one of my kids have an accident involving bodily fluids? Did my husband need my help? The woman held onto my hand, leading me from the back of the meeting room, where I was standing, into the lobby area. Was someone critically in need of prayer? Was a baby being born in the bathroom? Did someone leave a pumpkin latte out here with my name on it?

Instead of revealing any of those urgent situations, my friend pointed to the ceiling. "Look, see? The air-conditioning isn't cold. You have to get it fixed." I breathed a sigh of relief. "Oh! The air-conditioner? I don't know how to fix the air-conditioner. I barely know how to read a Celsius thermostat." She thought about this for a second and laughed. "But you *are* the pastor's wife."

Great and Fearful Expectations

Both my husband and I had wanted to minister overseas before we were married. My husband spent a summer in the Middle East and fell in love with the people, their culture, their language, and their food. Dave is constantly trying to come up with more ways to incorporate *shish tawook* into his diet. For my part, a few months after I began walking with God in college I read *Let the Nations Be Glad!* with some friends. If you've ever read this book by John Piper, then you know why I applied for a passport after finishing the first chapter.[2] I was excited to serve the Lord overseas and felt like I was ready to go yesterday. We began a five-year journey in seminary where both of us would earn degrees. We got married three weeks after beginning our first class in our first semester and took on multiple jobs to stay afloat. During breaks from classes we led numerous short-term overseas mission trips for college students. I was so excited to do ministry overseas and for my husband to be a church planter. It seemed especially sweet that we were given the opportunity to explore ministry opportunities abroad while we were still in seminary.

But despite my knowledge of how ministry was a privilege, there was one thing about all this that terrified me. I was certain that I would never be able to measure up to everyone's expectations. All over the world, wherever we traveled, it seemed that my fear of man was confirmed at every turn. "You know you have to homeschool if you go abroad," one missionary said. "You don't have much time left to learn how to read music," a pastor's wife warned me. "What your husband really needs most is a full belly of home-cooked meals and a thrilling sex life to keep him going," a book for ministry wives instructed. The churches we visited all over the world had so many varying ideas of what their pastor and his wife were to be about. Every time we came back from a whirlwind trip across the globe, my head would spin with the world of expectations—lead the women, step back and disciple others to lead the women; be attractive to please your husband, be demure and have a [literally] quiet voice; model godliness, model brokenness. Don't embarrass yourself and your husband through your ignorance, immaturity, or inexperience in ministry. And by all means, do everything in your power to keep your husband and children as godly as possible so that he will not be disqualified from the ministry. (Note: salvation is from the Lord, *not* the pastor's wife.)

I might have been too paralyzed to even pack my suitcase if I had taken all these ideas too seriously. Just thinking about expectations can make a minister's wife want to throw in the dish towel at the first potluck.

Where Does the Minister's Wife Fit In?

Our husbands need so much support, from studying in seminary to chairing elder meetings to organizing details for the church budget. We see them engaging in relationships with leaders in the community, visiting people in the hospital, praying on the phone with church members, sending e-mails to staff, and hunting for resources in the library. We're with them in the middle of much of this labor of love. It's easy to get caught up in the expectations and roles debate and leave it at that. But I think too many conversations regarding ministry wives are centered on who she is and what she ought to do, and we spend so little time talking about who Christ is and what he has done and will do. Discussions of our ideals and expectations are healthy and helpful insofar as they do not distract us from loving our Chief Shepherd, our husband, and the church whom Christ died to purchase for himself.

In case you don't have time to read the rest of this book I'll just put my cards on the table—I think wives of ministers need encouragement and refreshment in the Lord, and we find that hope and help in the gospel. This idea isn't new or scandalous, but with all the things clamoring for our attention I think we (I!) could use an opportunity to recalibrate our perspective and set our gaze on eternal things. After all, why would we want to wade around in shallow puddles of man-made ideals when there is the incomprehensible ocean of the love of Christ that surpasses all knowledge for us to dive into (Eph. 3:18–19)?

I can imagine that you might be thinking a variety of things as you read this, depending on your perspective of what a ministry wife should be. Perhaps something about the idea of having this role shaped by others' expectations unsettles you. But maybe you can't think of any realistic alternatives. After all, everyone has expectations placed upon them—everyone. A good question we ought to ask is this: Where are these expectations coming from? Frankly speaking, there are no verses that outline the expectations of the formal office of ministry wife because there is no such office prescribed in the Bible. The Bible does assume that some pastors will be married, so there are qualifications that such men (if they are married) be "married to one wife."[3] But there is no formal role for their wives detailed in Scripture. Despite the absence of this formal role in Scripture, many a ministry wife is viewed as a staff member, an honorary elder, and even a copastor. It's no wonder that ministry wives feel pressure and loneliness. I imagine that when most of us scan the landscape of ministry ahead, we are overwhelmed, and this is the predominant thought that comes to mind.

I have a lot of hopes for this book. I want to dig deep into what the Bible says about who we are, what ministry and the church are all about, and how God uses weak people to do his will on earth.

My prayer is that this book would be used to equip and encourage you. I realize that your time and energy are in high demand, so I want to honor that and drill down to the things that matter and let you draw out the implications for your unique life and ministry. I'm hoping that this resource is refreshing, because the grace of God can give us a humility that smiles rather than sweats when it comes to talking about the work of pastoral ministry. Speaking of not sweating the personal stuff, I should go turn on the fan in my room. Our air-conditioner might be broken again.

PART 1

Loving the
Chief Shepherd

1

"But You're the
Pastor's Wife"

Who am I? Where am I? What am I? Am I supposed to be
playing some sort of role? If so, where did I put that script?
And who wrote the screenplay? When we're not sure of
these things, we can find ourselves improvising in ways
that are less than satisfying (and even self-destructive).
This chapter lays the foundation and framework for a discussion on identity by talking about who God is and who
we are according to what the Bible says. Remembering
that we are redeemed sinners who are loved by a holy God
is a message we all need to be regularly reminded of. Our
identity at the most basic and fundamental level is that we
are "in Christ."

Lost and Then Found in Him:
on "Finding" That Our Identity Is in Christ

You're probably familiar with the children's game hide-and-seek. One of my sons loves this game, but he can't stand the suspense of the hunt. He stands somewhere out in the open and calls, "Here I am. Come get me!" Sometimes I "lose" my glasses even though they're right there on my face and fumble around in the bathroom looking for them. It may be comical to see a child hide in plain sight or watch someone rifle through toiletries looking for something they haven't lost. But it's less than humorous to watch Christians forget that they are "in Christ" and live out of some warped identity. We wander around like poor, lost sheep, bleating that nobody loves us; all the while we are actually safe forever in the arms of our Savior.

What do we mean when we say we need to find our identity in Jesus? Is our identity lost? It's important to think about these commonly used terms to discover the underlying meanings of what we're talking about. Living in a cross-cultural context has taught me time and again that we cannot assume we are communicating clearly even when speaking our own language. Further, even among fellow followers of Christ we have need for ongoing clarification.

What thoughts enter your mind when someone asks you, "Who are you?" Where you live or your nationality is what most people are looking for when they ask this question. Naturally, there is a host of connections and ideas that enter one's mind when you hear a country's name. For example, when one woman learned that I'm from the United States she said, "Ah, I know Americans. You are *Baywatch*!" What she saw on an internationally broadcast television show informed her view of my country and of me. This is an extreme (and extremely awkward) example, but I think we can all relate to this woman's thought process when we think of identity. We automatically connect whatever we know of the whole to the individual and vice versa. The ending to that interaction is that I fumbled my way through an explanation of Peter's introduction in his first letter "to those who are elect exiles of the Dispersion in Pontus, Galatia, Cappadocia, Asia, and Bithynia" (1 Pet. 1:1). My citizenship is in heaven (Phil. 3:20–21), so I am a Christian whose passport was issued by the United States government. I retain my cultural heritage, yet my primary identity is defined by God's uniting me to Jesus through his death and resurrection.

So, what is your identity? By what or by whom do you define yourself? Are you the master of your identity? Is your identity "lost in plain sight"? To call yourself a Christian is to embrace the cross of Jesus Christ and everything it says about who God is and who you are. You are in Christ. The fact that Jesus, the sinless Son of God, allowed himself to be crucified on a cross like a criminal says a lot of things. The cross says that God is utterly holy, and we are utterly sinful. The cross says that God requires a blood sacrifice for sins committed against him, and Jesus took this punishment in our place (Rom. 3:21–26). The cross says that God loves us in ways that we cannot comprehend (see Eph. 3:19). "In this is love, not that we have loved God but that he loved us and sent his Son to be the propitiation for our sins" (1 John 4:10). The cross says that God has provided the righteous standing we need to dwell in his holy presence and not die. "For our sake he made him to be sin who knew no sin, so that in him we might become the righteousness of God" (2 Cor. 5:21). Because of what Christ did for us on the cross, he has destroyed every obstacle that prevented us from enjoying him forever. Because of the cross we are no longer slaves but sons, and if sons, then heirs through God (Gal. 4:7). We are no longer strangers and aliens but fellow citizens with the saints and members of the household of God (Eph. 2:19). We are free in the most awe-filled, reverent, and joyful sense of the word. We apprehend these things by faith, which is a gift, so none of us can boast (Eph. 2:8–9).

Whenever we speak of our identity as being a woman, a wife, or a pastor's wife, let us have in our minds *the* primary reference point of being "found in him" (Phil. 3:9). Every hat we wear or role we play must be viewed through this perspective. Like the "lost" glasses that were right there on my face, your identity is always found in him whether or not you are conscious of it. This is why we need to rehearse the gospel often, asking the Spirit to transform us and remind us of God's truth (Rom. 12:2).

God, Man, Christ, Response

The identity question is one that we like to answer using labels. Sometimes the labels we use get more and more descriptive. "I'm the wife of ___," one woman says. Another may say, "I'm a mom." Then we tack on our personal peculiarities: "I'm a mom whose children are educated in such a way"; "I'm a mom who eats this kind of food"; "I'm a wife whose husband's role in the church is this"; "I'm a woman who treats her illnesses in this manner"; "I'm a mom whose child plays this game"; "I'm a woman who buys this brand of whatever"; et cetera. We like to think of ourselves in terms of what we consume, produce, or possess, or how we behave.

But being a Christian is neither a label nor an area of interest nor a matter of personal opinion. Being a Christian means that the most basic and fundamental thing about you has changed forever. No longer your own, you are now defined by *whose* you are. You were dead in your sins, and now you are alive to God. This reality of being in Christ is not something we conjure up in our imagination to quell our insecurities. Exactly how has it come about that we are now "found in him, not having a righteousness of [our] own that comes from the law, but that which comes through faith in Christ, the righteousness from God that depends on faith" (Phil. 3:9)? We must look to God's authoritative Word and not to our subjective feelings about how our heart feels today.

We like to create our own standards, but even our contrived standards are benign. We say things like, "At least

I'm not _____, like So-and-so." Subjective, halfhearted, and sometimes blended with biblical ideals, our standards are mere comparisons to other people. But God's Word tells us that we are not autonomous. We are accountable to God, who created us. In Romans 1 we learn that "the wrath of God is [being] revealed from heaven" (v. 18). We owe our Creator complete allegiance and heartfelt worship, but these things we have reserved exclusively for ourselves to our eternal demise. "For although they knew God, they did not honor him as God or give thanks to him, but they became futile in their thinking, and their foolish hearts were darkened" (Rom. 1:21). We are all under sin (Rom. 3:9). We don't have to search too far back in our memory to recall an occasion when we honored ourself above God or disregarded his grace toward us. We have no excuses—we've all broken God's law and deserve judgment. Our contrived standards and human laws cannot compare to God's holiness, and his wrath is righteously directed against all wickedness.

Every mouth is stopped—the whole world accountable to God (Rom. 3:19). "But now . . ." But! Now! "But now the righteousness of God has been manifested apart from the law, although the Law and the Prophets bear witness to it" (Rom. 3:21). God himself provided a way for us to escape the just penalty for our sin and be counted righteous before him. This forgiveness and righteous standing have absolutely nothing to do with how high we can pull ourselves up by our moral bootstraps. The bootstraps of self-righteousness are chains. This righteousness of God apart from the law is a gift of grace. It is only through trusting in the work of Christ's sacrificial death that we can be "justified by his grace as a gift" (Rom. 3:24). How do we get this gift? What do we do with this news? We respond to this good news through faith and *believe*. "And to the one who does not work but believes in him who justifies the ungodly, his faith is counted as righteousness" (Rom. 4:5).

As the wife of a man in ministry, you may be aware of the various expectations that people have of you. Your culture, family members, fellow church members, community, and certainly your husband have ideas about who you are to them and to others. Their ideas about who you are probably vary from person to person. Are you feeling overwhelmed? Be assured that the one whose so-called opinion matters most has *the* decisive word on your identity. When you hear of the expectations that others have of you, you are free to consider them in light of God's truth. There is ultimately no threat to your personhood, dignity, or worth, because the God who created all things, including you, does not have debatable opinions. Who you are in Christ never changes and is not threatened. God is the one whose name is "I AM WHO I AM" (Ex. 3:14), and he says, "Fear not, for I have redeemed you; I have called you by name, you are mine" (Isa. 43:1). We could not have been given a more thrilling identity! Does someone have an expectation of you that is true and noble and praiseworthy? You are free in Christ to walk in love toward those around you as you draw on his strength to serve. Does someone have an expectation of you that is not true, noble, or praiseworthy? You are free in Christ to walk in love toward those around you as you graciously decline. In either case there is no need for defensiveness, fear, anxiety, or insecurity but only for gracious rest because of our security in Christ.

Wake Up, Sleepyhead

Even as we are God's beloved whom he loves with a steadfast, everlasting love (Ps. 103:17), this massive, weighty truth just doesn't thrill our hearts 24-7. Consider the vast number of lectures we have attended, the sermons we have heard preached, and the Bible studies we've completed. Even so, we grow bored and irritated when we hear someone speak of God's love for us. "I already know that," we sigh. "Yeah, but. . ."—our hearts are dissatisfied. But in saying this, we reveal that we have actually forgotten. "I already believed the gospel; can we move on?" We shrug off the reminders. And again, we reveal that we have forgotten. Even in the midst of solid preaching, regular opportunities for outreach, days on end of fellowship gatherings, and all variety of religious activity, we can get bored of worship, ministry, and communion with God.

I'm sure you've experienced a season in which you sit down to read your Bible and pray but you can't keep your mind from wandering to all the other things you'd rather be doing. Lately I've been distracted by my hair (this is silly, I know). The air in our city changes from humid to arid quickly, and my hair doesn't like that. When I'm sitting still and want to quiet my heart, I find that I'm actually thinking about how uncomfortable I am in my own skin and hair. My mind also wanders to profuse and multiplying thoughts about myself. "Everyone is so selfish. No one has time to think of me," the ego complains. So I compensate for the attention deficit I feel and obsess over my plans, my feelings, and my stuff. I become the biggest thing in my mind, and my desires become the strongest tugs in my heart. Of course, this narcissistic disposition affects everyone around me. If I'm not happy, then nobody's happy. In reflecting on these times, I can feel my conscience sting from conviction of sin.

Perhaps you feel the same shame or frustration about feeling bored with God's love. If you hear the hissing accusations of Satan, who tells you that you're a self-centered sinner, then remind the Devil that he may be well aware of your sin, but because of Jesus your heavenly Father has promised to forget them all (Ps. 103:12). "I, I am he who blots out your transgressions for my own sake, and I will not remember your sins" (Isa. 43:25). Praise God for his indwelling Holy Spirit, who is kind to lead us away from sin and into righteousness. What a grace to know that something is awry when God's beautiful truth becomes blasé!

It's a gift to see the disparity between our affections for God and his utter worthiness, because then we see that God has not left us to ourselves but is reaching out to us in his kindness to repent of our sin. In these times we can see how ministry is an impetus to direct our affections to the Lord. Time and time again the women in our church have pointed me back to Christ as we walk together confessing this struggle to one another. I'm so thankful!

Lest we come to believe that the gospel and the resulting ministry of the gospel are about us, we need to behold our God. When we're being tugged in a navel-gazing direction, we need to behold our God. When we're anxious about the vision we had for our lives, we need to behold our God. When we're content with how life is going and feel little urgency about anything, much less spiritual matters, we need to behold our God! We need to have the eyes of our hearts enlightened so we may know the hope to which he's called us, our glorious inheritance, and the immeasurable greatness of his power toward us (Eph. 1:17–19). There is always more to life than what meets the physical eye. Every day and even every hour we need to wake up. In the short time it took you to read these few paragraphs, you are that many breaths closer to meeting the Lord face-to-face. We are careening toward our eternal destiny according to God's sovereign and good plans. "Besides this you know the time, that the hour has come for you to wake from sleep. For salvation is nearer to us now than when we first believed" (Rom. 13:11).

Do you use an alarm clock to wake up in the morning? I sometimes use the alarm on my mobile phone. There are dozens of options for the alarm sound! It's important to pick the right sound, right? You don't want to wake up to an obnoxious noise or miss the alarm because the sound is too soft to hear. What sort of thing will wake us up from our spiritual grogginess? We need to splash buckets of ice water on our sleepy souls when we're tempted toward the despising, despairing, or degrading of God's astonishing good news. "So then let us not sleep, as others do, but let us keep awake and be sober" (1 Thess. 5:6). God's sufficient Word peels back the façade we have drawn over the reality he has created. The reality check we need cannot be gained through "listening to our hearts" and telling ourselves who we are. Through God's Word we gain an eternal perspective through which we can evaluate every heart twinge, relationship, and circumstance. Do you know a timeless, familiar Bible verse that speaks to this? "Your word is a lamp to my feet and a light to my path" (Ps. 119:105). What mercy from God that he would give us his illuminating Word and that it is always shining, regardless of whether we perceive it.

Just Keep Swimming

Do you recall the way you felt as you walked down the aisle to stand by your husband at your wedding ceremony? The

35

church that my husband and I were married in had a very, *very* long aisle. It was nicknamed "the green mile" because of the green carpet. When they opened the back doors of the sanctuary, I could see the platform lit up way down the aisle at the front of the room. The glare of the lights and the distance made it so that I sort of had to take it by faith that everyone was in place and that Dave was standing there waiting for me. My father took my arm, and we started walking. At first I couldn't see my groom clearly, and everyone's gaze fixed on me made me feel nervous. But when we got closer and I locked eyes with Dave, he was all I could see. I remember feeling a swelling peace and joy fill my heart that crowded out my feelings of insecurity.

"Being married to a man in ministry means your life is in a fishbowl," a pastor's wife once told me, "because everyone is watching you." No doubt, there are elements of a life of ministry that resemble her remark. And there are biblical exhortations regarding discipleship that suggest that the people whom you are leading ought to be able to watch your life (2 Thess. 3:7–9; 2 Tim. 3:10; Heb. 13:7). This fishbowl illustration has truthful elements in it, and it is certainly a good thing to know that one is accountable to walk in integrity because people are watching your life. There is a safety and assurance that our family experiences in knowing that we are cared for enough by our church body and elders not to be ignored when it comes to keeping watch over our souls. But I think sometimes the fishbowl feeling can take a sinister tone—like your family is the fish in the tank and everyone else is a cat. They're watching you, waiting for an opportunity to strike.

I remember feeling this way when we first moved to the region of the world where we now live. My husband and I and our daughter lived across the border in a small town in a neighboring country. Everything was new—language, food, geography, customs, and lifestyle. Each day that I stepped out of our gate and walked around the corner to my language class, I was aware of the eyes that were watching me. Some stared openly and didn't look away when I noticed them. Others went out of their way to cross the street so they could cross paths with me and watch me walk to class. One time I entered a store and recognized the phrase spoken by the shopkeeper to another customer in their local dialect: "Look! There she is." All this attention made me uneasy, and I began to feel a strong desire to withdraw and avoid leaving my home. So I talked about my feelings with an older woman who had lived there for years. She explained that my neighbors with their stares weren't malicious but curious. "Why not let your light shine?" she encouraged me. This shifted my thinking, and I began to see multiple opportunities every day to speak to curious people about Jesus.

Sometimes we think of letting our light shine before others (Matt. 5:16) like it is a fireworks show. We need to keep the people ooh-ing and ahh-ing in new and surprising ways while we impress them with our astonishing godliness and perfections. But letting your light shine before others has an entirely different scope and aim. Our good deeds and upright conduct are not about showboating ourselves but about demonstrating that we have a better possession and a lasting one in heaven and that our Rescuer is both holy and forgiving.

God does not apologize to us for calling us to participate in his Great Commission, because it is an inestimable privilege. While we might imagine ourselves as the sole, lonely fish in the bowl, we can take comfort knowing that our church body is actually swimming with us. One of the reasons I love my diverse, multiethnic church is that we are united to one another in Christ—we are "we." Though we come from all over the world, there is no "they" in the body of Christ. We are a body! My heart is comforted week after week in our corporate worship gatherings as I look around and think, "We're together." I'm not alone! Sister, even in the hard-to-reach places of this world where the loneliness is not imagined but very real, we can still take heart because of the gospel. The weariness we feel when we look at all the needs around us is replaced by an invigorating appreciation for Jesus's performance on our behalf and his strength toward those who are weak. Grateful to God for grace, we pursue holiness and do our good works through his strength so that our Father in heaven gets the glory. We're all swimming together by God's grace alone.

2

On Inheriting a Kingdom of Idols and Expectations

Expectations can sneak up on you and surprise you when you least expect them. We can laugh about this moment now, but at the time it was very confusing for all of us. One year just before the Christmas Eve service began, a group of ladies gathered around me with disapproving looks on their faces. Someone spoke for the group, "This is not right. You are the pastor's wife! You are supposed to be the best-dressed woman here. *This is your night!* Where is your jewelry?" In an attempt to spare me from what she thought was a shame, she began to take her own necklace off to give me. My friends inherited this idea from their church's subculture back in their home country. It's just one of the things that everyone always knew—the pastor's wife is supposed to be the glitziest gal at the Christmas Eve gala. Christmas Eve was "her night" to strut her stuff. In my heart I was tempted with this opportunity to garner attention and praise.

It may seem odd to take this example of an expectation seriously. But grant me this—perhaps our expectations that are not congruent with Scripture have more in common with this example than we care to admit. This leads us to some questions to consider: Why are we so prone to setting up false expectations for ourselves or for others? What is it about us that makes us eager to go after false expectations and try to satisfy them? To answer these questions, we need to look at the heart issue behind all our sinful impulses: idolatry.

From Icons to Idols

My friend Bev grew up in a family that practiced the worship of ancestors and idols. When she was twelve years old her father marched out their back door carrying an axe. Bev's father laid into the statue of Buddha that was standing in their yard. The three-foot-tall, red, wooden statue was allegedly protecting them and giving their family good luck, but her father no longer believed that lie. He chopped the idol into smithereens while his daughter looked on in amazement. The Chaos had taught their daughters to revere the idol—*don't touch it, don't play with it, treat it with respect*. But when Bev's dad became a Christian, he dismantled and destroyed their household god in obedience to the one true God. "You shall have no other gods before me" (Ex. 20:3). His slavery to superstition and ancestor worship had been broken. Instead of looking to a piece of wood for things that only God can provide, Mr. Chao began to lead his family in trusting Christ.

The inclination toward idolatry is the natural posture of the human heart. It's the reason for every sin. You don't need to have a statue in your yard to serve an idol. When Satan tempted Adam and Eve in the garden he told them, "You will be like God" (Gen. 3:5). Martyn Lloyd-Jones summarized the problem of idolatry like this:

> This is the very essence of the biblical message, that man and woman, placed by God in a state of paradise and perfection, felt that even paradise was an insult to them because there was subjection to God. . . . Men and women were really meant to live a life in communion with God, and that happiness, in a full and final sense, is only really possible when they obey the law of their own being; and that as long as they refuse to do that, they can experience nothing but turmoil and unhappiness and wretchedness.[4]

After our first parents sinned, every human then imagined himself to be better off in slavery to self-worship. Mankind was meant to be an *icon*, a picture of what God is like as we display his image to the world. Instead, in our sin we became our own *idols*. We worship ourselves and expect others to do the same. Think about it—we are kind to the people who are kind to us. We boast in our strength and accomplishments. We envy those who have the strength and accomplishments we desire. We are rude to people who do not praise us. We insist on our own way. We are easily annoyed and resent those who don't acknowledge our sovereignty. We are ecstatic when our rivals stumble. We put up with people so far as they benefit us. In our minds we are the only ones who are truly praiseworthy, and we'll be damned if anyone should suggest otherwise. Ironically, we are duped into thinking that by these practices and heart postures we are liberated and independent, but really we are slaves. In chapter 1 we looked at Romans 1:21, "For although they knew God, they did not honor him as God or give thanks to him, but they became futile in their thinking, and their foolish hearts were darkened." Paul goes on to say in verse 25, "because they exchanged the truth about God for a lie and worshiped and served the creature rather than the Creator, who is blessed forever! Amen." We don't want to serve the creature anymore. We want to worship God! Is it too late to return the lie we bought in exchange for God's truth?

In Acts 17:29–31 Paul tells us the answer we are looking for:

> Being then God's offspring, we ought not to think that the divine being is like gold or silver or stone, an image formed by the art and imagination of man. The times of ignorance God overlooked, but now he commands

all people everywhere to repent, because he has fixed a day on which he will judge the world in righteousness by a man whom he has appointed; and of this he has given assurance to all by raising him from the dead.

Hallelujah! We have a rescuer! This man is not like the first man, Adam, who forsook God to worship himself. *No*. This is the God-man Jesus Christ, the last Adam, the only man who worshiped God with all his heart, soul, and mind, and loved his neighbor as he loved himself (Matt. 22:36–40). Whereas all of us were made sinners by Adam's disobedience, as many who call on Christ to save them will be made righteous by his obedience (Rom. 5:12–21). Our idolatry is forgiven, and our righteous standing before God is imputed to us by faith in the last Adam. The resurrection of Jesus Christ proves that God will keep his promise of canceled sin for all those whose trust is in his Son. When we trust that Jesus has secured our future of never-ending joy in him, we experience the power of the resurrected Christ who frees us from idolatry. Never again can we happily serve another god, because no god can satisfy us like the fullness we receive from Christ. So now we take up the axe of God's Word and strike into the root of our idols.

The Shackles of Ministry?

When we first moved to the Arabian Peninsula to help start a church planting movement, we had no idea if that plan would ever come to fruition. Nobody had formally invited us, and there were no positions to be filled. That was a faith-stretching time. When the uncertainty of it all would hit me afresh, I would feel the stress coursing through my body. "If this doesn't work, what would we *do*?" was a question I asked myself on a regular basis. "The Plan" for church planting was my functional idol, and I couldn't fathom what life would be like if the plan failed.

Serving alongside your husband in ministry may present you with great temptation toward idolatry. Some temptations are greater than others, and aspects of ministry may also become temptations to sin. All of us are vulnerable to temptation. "None is righteous, no, not one; no one understands; no one seeks for God" (Rom. 3:10–11).

Perhaps all this idol talk is new to you. Or maybe you're well familiar with these ideas. No doubt, at some point in your life someone has pointed out an idol to you. "All you ever talk about is ___ " and "The only thing you care about is ___ " are tools for our discernment in the hands of a gracious God. An offended party may have aimed these accusations at your heart to hurt you, but God can use these flashlights to show you falsehood. And when we see the idols masquerading as God in our hearts, we are taught to "fear God" (Prov. 1:7) because we have nothing to fear. "There is no fear in love, but perfect love casts out fear. For fear has to do with punishment, and whoever fears has not been perfected in love" (1 John 4:18). Our punishment for idolatry was borne in Christ's body on the cross. And it bears repeating over and over again—Jesus's perfect record of always worshiping the Father with his everything and never having other gods before the Father is ours through faith. Our job is to believe in him whom the Father sent (John 6:29) and rest in the finished work of Christ. We don't take up the axe to chop down our idols so that our Father will love us. No, we reject our idols *because* we are our Father's beloved daughters.

So how do you know if a ministry-related thing has usurped the place of God in your life? When has a ministry activity, accomplishment, or title become more important in your heart than God? What about ministry seems to give your life meaning or worth? What activity, if it were taken from you, would devastate you?[5] You know that a ministry opportunity is greater to you than Jesus if, when it is taken, hindered, or altered, you feel rattled, wrecked, preoccupied, anxious, insecure, insignificant, ignored, angry, sad, betrayed, or distraught. You would see no reason to be disturbed over the loss of that privilege to serve Jesus unless you had given it more value in your eyes than the pleasure of knowing Christ Jesus your Lord. When that happens, it is a hint that this thing may have become your idol. When we design our lives around our idols, we are setting up our own little kingdoms in which we insist that we are sovereign. When something or someone comes along and steps over the boundaries of our little kingdom, we get defensive. Our well-being is being threatened.[6]

Bowing Down to Ministry and Tribe

Perhaps you feel that without your church, you are nothing. Or, without you, your church is nothing. Either way, there is an unhealthy codependence in which your identity and livelihood are wrapped up in serving in ministry. Thoughts or statements like, "This church needs us," or "We can't lose this job," bubble to the surface of your mind. You may also feel that you have something very special to contribute to the people you serve, because, *bless their hearts*, they just don't get it like you do. "It's a good thing that we're here to lead these people," and "We are the ones who know how to teach the gospel so they'll hear it," may come to mind. Even though ministry and gospel resurgence are very good things, they are not God, and they would be happy for us to worship them instead. And our idol-manufacturing hearts would be happy to oblige. Do you feel you *must* have this ministry to be happy? Perhaps you cannot imagine your life without it or without your church (I can relate—I love my church!). But can you imagine still having a life?

Or maybe you're not so impressed with the ministry or the philosophy of ministry per se, but your heart is set on the people. For some of us, life only has meaning if the people (perhaps the women in particular) are happy to follow us, socialize with us, prioritize our friendship over others, and bless us with their glowing approval. The inner ring of socialites is like a holy of holies to us; it is sacred and must be left undisturbed. We go to great lengths to protect our reputation among them. What if they knew our weakness and sin? Our husband's weaknesses and sins? Would it still be "well with my soul" if we let the church leaders know that we need their prayer and support, for whatever reason? Do you need to enjoy the approval of the leaders in your church in order to enjoy life? Do you feel burdened to represent your husband and family as a public relations manager would? Does the social fallout of a disagreement among the ladies at church scare you? Isn't it a grace to us, then, when we are passed over for whatever reason, and when our opinion is ignored or marginalized in that women's ministry meeting, and when our child throws a fit in the middle of Communion? The idols of approval and power fall hard, and the aftershock of losing someone's approval echoes into all the empty spaces of our hearts. The power they wield is so great that they can turn our thoughts toward replaying conversations, scrutinizing relationships, and worrying about what other people are thinking.

But Jesus!

When Jesus canceled the record of debt that stood against us with its legal demands, he nailed it to the cross. Paid in full! Through his work on the cross Jesus disarmed the rulers and authorities and put them to open shame by triumphing over them (Col. 2:14-15). Idols are forever disgraced as worthless, powerless, and petty. When we live for our ministry, our ideological tribe, the inner circle at the ladies' ministry, or our followers, we are always left wanting. An idol can't die for our sins. Furthermore, when we fail our fans or our good reputation, these things will punish us. Idols do not give grace; they rule by karma.

But Jesus—he delivers us from going after false gods. Tasting and seeing Jesus is the expulsive, new affection that drives out our love affair with our idols. Jesus must be more fascinating to us than any new ways of living. Jesus must be more compelling to us than any opportunity. Jesus must be more familiar to us than any temporary circumstances. Jesus must be more valuable to us than any trinket or toy. Jesus must be more real to us than any fleeting self-image or narcissistic self-actualization. Jesus Christ liberates us; he is the one who breaks the power that idols have in our lives. God is faithful to unite our divided heart to fear his name (Ps. 86:11). Idols are harsh masters that demand our loyalty, strength, emotional attachment, and our money. Idols take life; Jesus gives life. Idols deceive us; God's Word is truth. The world reinforces our idols; the gospel exposes our idols. We must learn to discern our idols, and by God's grace we must forsake them and watch them topple over. When we treasure the gospel and see how Christ frees us from our idols, we will turn the world upside down (see Acts 17:6).

There Is Always One Expectation You Can Meet

If we truly knew all the expectations that others have of us, it would paralyze us. But there is one expectation we can have of ourselves that will free us. We must expect that we are always dependent on God's grace (and so is everyone else). The more our failures and weaknesses can point us to this one great expectation, the better. In pointing us to the cross, our frailties and shortcomings become servants for our joy in Christ.

A woman once approached me with this confession: "So many times you have disappointed me and do not work to please me as my pastor's wife." I was startled by, yet appreciative of, her brutal honesty. Then she continued, "And now I'm beginning to realize that you are not here to please me. All of us exist to please the Lord." In that moment I was acutely aware of the two very different ways her comments could affect me. My emotions could careen back and forth between being disturbed and angry by her audacious implied claim on my life, or I could see this as an opportunity to agree with her about my inadequacy to please everyone and the sufficiency of Jesus in our lives. We both can rejoice in Christ together because we both are utterly dependent on grace. By God's grace I said (and meant), "Well said, sister!" Then we enjoyed fellowship over this Scripture: "Whatever you do, work heartily, as for the Lord and not for men, knowing that from the Lord you will receive the inheritance as your reward. You are serving the Lord Christ" (Col. 3:23–24). As I recall this conversation with my sister, which could have been a relational stumbling block, I am overwhelmed with the truth that there is no fear in love

(1 John 4:18). It is so deeply edifying to have honest conversations like this at the foot of the cross.

I have to remind myself of this truth all the time: there is no people pleasing, no inner circle of exclusive relationships, and no ministry that can hold a candle to the joy of fellowship with God. There is no gift from men that compares to the inheritance we will receive from God. There's an eternity of unhindered fellowship with God right around the corner! We have an inheritance that is "imperishable, undefiled, and unfading, kept in heaven for [us]" (1 Pet. 1:4). Our church and ministry are released from the shackles of existing to make us feel okay or useful or important. Life is so short, and God is so desirable, why would we ever want to waste time making good things into idols? If only we could keep this single-minded perspective in all our relationships, expectations, and ministry opportunities! The love of God would cast out all our fear, freeing us to love each other. And one day this will be so—all the time and forever. Our fellowship with God and with one another will be perfect and unending.

"Though you do not now see [Jesus], you believe in him and rejoice with joy that is inexpressible and filled with glory, obtaining the outcome of your faith, the salvation of your souls" (1 Pet. 1:8–9). A day is coming when we will finally be free from slaving for our idols. Jesus gives us a glimpse of what this will be like: "Then the King will say to those on his right, 'Come, you who are blessed by my Father, inherit the kingdom prepared for you from the foundation of the world'" (Matt. 25:34). When we see Jesus's face, and he welcomes us into his rest, our affections for our idols will be gone forever. Until then we must pursue righteousness, godliness, faith, love, steadfastness, and gentleness as we fight the good fight, taking hold of the eternal life to which we were called (1 Tim. 6:11–12). The gospel frees us to enjoy fellowship with God (most of all!) and with each other. There is so much we can enjoy about our brothers and sisters, even now while we still struggle with sin—what grace! And amid all the expectations that come from others (and from yourself), expect that God's grace will always be sufficient for you all (2 Cor. 12:9).

3

Stay Close to Your
Shepherd, Little Sheep

It's kind of a joke to say that if you don't know the answer to a question in Sunday school, then just answer, "Jesus." Nine times out of ten you could be right. One time while we were in line at a store, I asked my daughter if she could help me pass something to the cashier. She must have been daydreaming, because when she realized that I had asked her a question she blurted out her go-to answer: "Jeee-sus!"

The idea of prioritizing your relationship with God is kind of like the Sunday-school answer. "What is my main priority?" our heart wonders. "Love God first," the Sunday-school answer chimes in. We know this. It's not a hard question to answer. When something profound becomes commonplace like this, it can seem trite. But, actually, loving God first and foremost is the most awe-filled and mysterious thing to which we could possibly endeavor. In this final chapter on loving the Chief Shepherd, I hope to remind you of the unfathomable magnitude of this simple Sunday-school answer.

He's Got You and Me, Sister, in His Hand

Your relationship with God is not by your own doing. You were the lost sheep, and he, the seeking shepherd. Scattered across the globe over the ages of human history is the flock of God whom he foreknew and predestined to be conformed to the image of his Son. But when the fullness of time had come, God sent forth his Son, born of a woman, born under the law (Gal. 4:4). This Son would be the Good Shepherd of the sheep. The Good Shepherd is not a disinterested hired hand who cares nothing for the sheep but only for his own skin. He is the one shepherd foretold in Ezekiel: "As a shepherd seeks out his flock when he is among his sheep that have been scattered, so will I seek out my sheep, and I will rescue them from all places where they have been scattered on a day of clouds and thick darkness" (Ezek. 34:12; see also vv. 23–24). Isaiah spoke of his kindness: "He will tend his flock like a shepherd; he will gather the lambs in his arms; he will carry them in his bosom, and gently lead those that are with young" (Isa. 40:11).

Jesus will never lose any of his sheep; no one will snatch them out of his hand (John 10:28–29). He gave you this grace even before you were born, before the world was created, indeed, *before the ages began* (2 Tim. 1:8–10). Did you think that loving God was your own idea, based on your own initiative? Is your ongoing relationship with the Lord sustained by your interest in his Word, or your passion for prayer, or your inclination toward holiness? None of these things are our own doing—they are gifts. If God always makes the first move and finishes what he starts, would he then leave the middle up to us? Grace carries us all the way through. The green pastures, the still waters, the rod and staff, the oil—all these things are provided by our Shepherd. Let the truth of his deliberate grace comfort you.

Sister, if the Lord is your shepherd, he will not leave you wanting. He provides abundantly for your needs and cares for you in seasons that are frightening. Of all the things we need on this earth, he provides it all, *and* he restores our *soul*. There is no shadow in any valley so dark that his Word does not illumine. Sister, you're being followed. "Surely goodness and mercy shall follow me all the days of my life, and I shall dwell in the house of the LORD forever" (Ps. 23:6). Held in our Shepherd's unflinching grip, we are safely his at all times and in every circumstance. Your constancy is Christ. And at the end of all things created, in the most beautiful paradox of the ages, the Lamb is shown to be the Shepherd, "and he will guide them to springs of living water, and God will wipe away every tear from their eyes" (Rev. 7:17).

Don't You Love the Way He Loves You?

A friend of mine has a sister who is suffering from dementia. As her body struggles against aging and disease, her mental faculties are shutting down at an accelerated pace. Because of the illness, she hardly recognizes her loved ones anymore and does not know who she is. There is unspeakable grief and pain surrounding these circumstances, yet in all of this heartbreak there is hope and peace. Although she doesn't know who she is, *God knows her*. She's a Christian—one who has been grafted into Christ by faith through grace. In the absence of her self-awareness and awareness of others, God is ever aware of her. Made in God's image, her heartbeat, breath, and brain waves testify to God's mercy. He foreknew her, predestined her to be conformed to the image of his Son, made her in his own image, called her to himself, led her to repentance and faith, justified her by the blood of Jesus, and glorified her forever as his adopted daughter.

Failing mental faculties and diminishing physical abilities—neither can separate us from the love of God that is in Christ Jesus. Even while she has no idea what is going on, God still maintains his love to her every second of every day now and forever. She is utterly *loved*. And her Savior is able to save her to the uttermost since he always lives to make intercession for her (Heb. 7:25). This is shocking because it means that God's steadfast love for his children is ultimately not dependent on them. He doesn't lose interest in those who can't express interest in him anymore. His steadfast love isn't diminished because she can't serve or teach or lead. God's faithfulness is inextricably who he is. He *is* faithful.

We would do well to consider what this means for our lives and endeavor to remember it every day. We need to remember that God's grand vision for our lives starts with him and is for his glory. It makes sense that if we want to make it our chief aim to love the Chief Shepherd, then we must start with who he is and what he has done on our behalf. When we start with ourselves, we are caught up in ourselves, our quirks, our misgivings, and the ways we would prefer God to love us.

Compared to our shadowy self-love, the love of God is permanently resolute. All the so-called *self-realization* we seek is shown to be petty compared to being known by God. *Self-sufficiency* comes undone in the presence of the Holy One in whom all things hold together, and our *self-righteousness* reeks like rotten fruit. When light is cast on the rock-solid fortress of the eternal security we have in Christ, our *self-assurance* slinks into the shadows. Our insecure *self-defense* has nothing novel to say, because our heavenly Father is in charge of our public relations department. Through the power of the Holy Spirit, all the energy absorbed by our *self-awareness* becomes readily available for Christlike sacrificial love. Being aware of these spiritual realities that play out in our lives is a source of sweet joy.

Our hearts are strengthened by joy, God is glorified in our dependence on him, and the watching world becomes curious about the reason for our hope.

Being known and loved by God—being found *in Christ*—has far-reaching implications for our lives. Through his death and resurrection, Jesus has resolved every obstacle that prevented us from treasuring God forever. Eternity is an eternity long because we need forever in order to experience and enjoy the love of God. Paul prayed that God would give us "strength to comprehend" the love of Christ in all its breadth, length, height, and depth (Eph. 3:18–19). Oh, how he loves us!

All Things Are Yours

One—*just one*—of the ways God loves us is that he names us as heirs of his kingdom. Consider the vast magnitude of the love God has toward those who are his. Everything exists for God. "For by him all things were created, in heaven and on earth, visible and invisible, whether thrones or dominions or rulers or authorities—all things were created through him and for him" (Col. 1:16). "All things" encompasses a great deal—precisely, *everything*. God's happy sovereignty over our life, marriage, family, and ministry is fuel for our joy. Because God's will for our sanctification is inextricably tied to our happiness in him, we have nothing to fear. "The Father loves the Son and has given all things into his hand" (John 3:35). We serve an unimpeachable king, and he loves us with an everlasting love. If Christ is God's and you are Christ's, then all things are yours through Christ (1 Cor. 3:21–23). Nothing in life or death can separate you from his love, and he is working all things together for your good (Rom. 8:28–39). This world and everything related to this life, your physical death (which is inevitable), your present circumstances (good and bad), and your future (uncertain as it may seem)—all are working together for your good. In the hands of our redeemer, they are servants of joyful hope, not futile hopelessness. In the hands of almighty God all these things are your midwives, by your side, helping to bring forth holiness and renewal of spirit even now in this present dark age before the Son returns. Everything exists for God, and all things are his servants (Ps. 119:89–91) employed in his business of bringing about his gospel good in your life.

Our boasting in ourselves is kind of like when my children and I get into an elevator with other people. Invariably, a fellow elevator passenger leans over the stroller and adores the baby. One of my daughters will say, "Yup. That's *my* baby brother. He's *mine*. *My* brother. I'm his big sister." She's proud of him, and she's proud to be a big sister— which I think is wonderful. But she didn't do anything to receive her role as a big sister. It was given to her freely. There's no work she could have done to earn him. She has only to receive the joy that he is her baby brother and enjoy him, as he is such a delight.

Similarly, we have no grounds to boast in ourselves in our role as a ministry wife, mother, teacher, employee, boss, or whatever. We have no grounds to boast in our gifts, skills, talents, and opportunities. We don't boast in any of these things because *we don't need to*. "So let no one boast in men. For all things are yours" (1 Cor. 3:21). God has given us everything in Christ to enjoy, and he has given it all freely because of Jesus. "We get everything upon the credit of [Jesus's] name, and because not only has our unworthiness ceased to be recognized by God in his dealings with us, but our demerit been supplanted by the merit of One who is absolutely and divinely perfect."[7] So, boasting in stuff, gifts, roles, and people is a moot point. Our inheritance in Christ Jesus also establishes a moratorium on envy. Richard Sibbes said in his book *Glorious Freedom*:

> In spiritual things there is no basis for envy, for everyone may partake of everything. In the things of this life there is envy, because the more one has, the less another has. But for more to partake of spiritual things is a matter of glory and excellency.[8]

Because of Christ, all we know is grace. And from his fullness we have all received grace upon grace (John 1:16). In the end, we do boast. Indeed, we can't help but boast. We brag on our elder brother, who left his Father's house to come and seek us out and redeem us from the pigsty we were wallowing in. We are received with joy and adopted as daughters in our Father's house. We were once dead but are alive again; we were lost but have been found. We boast in God, who is mighty to save.

Amen. Come, Lord Jesus!

There is a joyful celebration before the angels of God over one sinner who repents (Luke 15:10). The wedding feast has been scheduled since before the ages began, and we hope for that day because it is a sure thing. Loving our Chief Shepherd means we look to his coming and pray for its speedy arrival. Jesus assures us in Revelation 22:20, "He who testifies to these things says, 'Surely I am coming soon.' Amen. Come, Lord Jesus!" But while we remain here waiting for our heavenly bridegroom to come for us, we must walk by faith. As we walk by faith, we groan inwardly as we wait eagerly for our adoption and the redemption of our bodies. The whole creation, actually, has been groaning together in the pains of childbirth (Rom. 8:22–23).

The childbirth imagery suggests urgent focus and ex-pectancy on our part. If you have experienced spontaneous labor in childbirth, then pondering that thought may bring back a flood of memories (and perhaps a surge of adrena-line). One psychological benefit of labor pains is that one can know the body is being prepared for imminent birth. When my youngest child was born almost two weeks early within only a few minutes' notice, I missed having the men-tal and emotional preparation to receive our child and hold him in my arms. Thankfully, my husband was at home and acted quickly to catch the baby and call my doctor and an ambulance for help. Both the baby and I were fine, praise the Lord! The postpartum recovery time was bumpy, partly because of the shock of giving birth in conditions that I had never anticipated. God's grace was sufficient for that recovery (and now we have a crazy story of a baby born in two contractions).

The labor pains and the groaning Paul talks about in Romans 8 are anticipatory and burgeoning with hope. It reminds us that something is on the verge, something is in process. Have no qualms about it: we *are* being prepared for something that we can hardly comprehend. Like labor pains, there is a goal and an end to our groaning. We groan in the hope of seeing God's glory. Jesus is coming—*he is coming*. Of this we can rest assured. We do not labor in vain. As a birth doula, I've had the privilege of accompanying many mothers in the labor room. I remember on one occasion after a mother experienced the first of many powerful muscle contractions, she looked at me and said, "This just got real." Her labor was certainly real before then, but the onset of contractions that engulfed her signaled that she needed to focus. I could hear in her voice and see in her demeanor that she was ready—*focused and ready*.

We are groaning yet ever expectant; we are sorrowful yet always rejoicing. Our eyes are on our Chief Shepherd. As I finish up this chapter, it is Christmastime. During this season people in the West are bombarded with crèches of our Savior. Perhaps you can hear in your heart the words of the hymn playing on my iTunes this morning:

> O come, all ye faithful, joyful and triumphant!
> O come ye, O come ye to Bethlehem;
> Come and behold him
> Born the King of Angels:
> O come, let us adore Him,
> Christ the Lord.[9]

Bethlehem, "house of bread," was home to the little shepherd boy named David who later became a king. Generations later, once again, Bethlehem became the birthplace of *the* king. This king was the bread of life and our Chief Shepherd.

The Holy One, whose throne is wrapped in lightning, took our depravity into his own body on the tree. Burdened by our evil, Jesus bore the infinitely horrifying wrath of the Father as he took the punishment for our sin. In Christ's death on the cross, our decrepit deadness to joy also died. Through faith in Jesus we're not blind to God's beauty anymore. Our joy in God—this unending joy of unparalleled heights—was planned for us since before the ages began. We can be assured that this joy is ours forever because Jesus purchased it explicitly for us with his precious blood. In the wake of grace we cannot but help love back the one who first loved us. We are prone to wander still, but now, by the Spirit who dwells within us, we are free to delight in the superior love of God. Now, God is about his ongoing work in us, both to will and to work for his good pleasure (Phil. 2:13). In all the storms where our hearts feel tossed about and drenched with despair, we can trace through the rain the rainbow of God's promise of future grace. God is at work for his purposes, and he will keep us through any and all affliction. The valley of the shadow of death is as dark as it is deep, but the Good Shepherd will lead us confidently through it all until he brings us to our inheritance: pleasure in God's presence for eternity (Ps. 16:11).

This king does not want merely our heart. Jesus has given us life through giving us his very life on the cross. Overflowing with thankfulness, we give him back the life he has given us. We love the Lord with all our heart, mind, soul, and strength. In a word, we are to love the Lord with our *everything*. All other loves are subject to our first love—the Chief Shepherd.

PART 2

Loving an
Under-Shepherd

4

On Doing Him Good
(and Not Harm)

Our minivan rumbled onto the driveway of the hotel where our church meets, and I hopped out to run around the front of the car to open the passenger door. My husband stepped out of the van, waved to our kids in the backseat, and disappeared into the crowd walking into the hotel. As I slid back into the driver's seat of the car, I laughed to myself. I never imagined that I would serve as a chauffeur to my pastor. I had leaned over him to buckle his seat belt, jogged around the van to get his door before the drivers behind us got impatient, and handed him his Bible and sermon notes at an angle that he can easily manage. I know we look comical—people always stare. But I also know that what looks awkward to others is graceful in the eyes of God. I do all this because my husband needs my help, as he suffers from a nerve disorder that causes him chronic pain and physical disabilities.

We all have ideas in our mind about how we want to serve in ministry. We might take personality inventories and spiritual-gift questionnaires looking for a bulleted list of things to do or at least an explanation of the way God made us. When facing a ministry task we ask ourselves, "How do I prefer to help? What did God make me to do?" And we seek out that thing. But sometimes that thing doesn't look quite like we imagined. The list of needs in the church bulletin doesn't seem to match our experience. The ministry that lands on our doorstep is unfamiliar, and we feel ill equipped. The task at hand is uncomfortable or painful. Or perhaps the opportunity to love others through a particular service is just not as exciting as the opportunity over *there* that *she* has. There may be a smorgasbord of ministries that you could be involved in—children's ministry, homeless ministry, music team, parking lot greeters, making-sure-everyone-gets-their-dishes-back-after-the-potluck team, and the list goes on. Even in the midst of all these opportunities to serve, wives of men in ministry have a God-given calling and enablement to serve their husband. In this chapter I hope to share some encouragement from God's Word to encourage you in your Albert ministry, Rajesh ministry, Huang ministry, Dave ministry, or Mahmoud ministry.

On Being a Helper

"Someone please come and help in here," I called from inside the kitchen to where my children were, running their nightly obstacle course of activity through our apartment.

My preschool son wandered in. "Whatchoo need, Mommy?" "Hey, buddy, can you put these wet clothes in the dryer?" I opened the washing machine for him to empty. Then I turned around to open the dishwasher so I could take out the clean dishes and put them away.

At the sound of the clanking glasses, he whirled on his heels and declared, "Ooh! I'm a big helper for the dishes!"

Because handling glasses and knives isn't a good chore for my swashbuckling preschooler, I declined. "No, I want you to put the clothes in the dryer. That will help Mommy."

But he wasn't hearing any of that, because the dishes were so shiny and the wet clothes were so boring. In honest preschool style, he got upset because I wouldn't let him unload the dishwasher. I can totally relate. My heart is the same as my child's. *I want to help, I really do! But, Lord, you want me to help* how?

The Bible describes wives as their husband's "helper." That has been our role from the beginning, since creation. "Then the LORD God said, 'It is not good that the man should be alone; I will make him a helper fit for him'" (Gen. 2:18). "Helper" is a role, and a role that God uses to describe himself. For various reasons there are some who read the Genesis passage and reject the idea of the wife being created to be the husband's helper. This is a guess based on my limited experience, but I think that what people tend to dislike about it is the assertion that the wife is uniquely the helper of the husband. Speaking for myself, I think in my own moments of struggling with this creation mandate, it's not so much that I don't want to be the helper of my husband. I *do* want to help him, but what I feel anxious about is who's going to help *me*? My husband is a busy church planter, we have four young children, we live in a foreign culture, and my husband has physical disabilities that limit what he is able to do for himself (and others) physically. As I talk with other wives in ministry I discover that I am not alone in my feelings. Generally, we feel honored that God would unite us to our husband and set us apart as "a helper fit for him." We delight in serving and blessing our husband. But at the beginning of a long weekend of church-related activities, in the middle of the busy work of everyday life, and at the end of an exhausting season, if we feel bitterness in our hearts then we can likely trace it back to this doubt: "What about me? Where's *my* help, Lord?"

I've come to learn that getting more help around the house, or having less physical pain or fewer loads of laundry, can hardly fix a problem that fundamentally has to do with the heart. When the posture of your heart is not one of humble submission to the Chief Shepherd's sovereign will, everyone else's grass looks greener. Where does your help come from? A lighter schedule? A babysitter? A bigger budget? Perhaps those things will bring temporary relief. Moses certainly benefited from his father-in-law's advice about delegation to lighten his workload (Ex. 18:14). The Bible tells us that our enduring and ultimate help comes from the Lord: "I lift up my eyes to the hills. From where does my help come? My help comes from the LORD, who made heaven and earth" (Ps. 121:1–2). You are not without help in your ministry to your husband.

Consider the incredible connection between the instruction and promises in Hebrews 13:5–6 and our ministry to our husband:

> Keep your life free from love of money, and be content with what you have, for he has said, "I will never leave you nor forsake you." So we can confidently say, "The Lord is my helper; I will not fear; what can man do to me?"

The writer of Hebrews calls to mind specific promises from the Old Testament (Joshua 1:5; Ps. 56:4, 11; 118:6), quotes them, and brings them to bear on our lives. This logic is astounding. Because the Lord is our helper, we do not fear. Because God promises to always be with his children, we should be content and make sure to keep money in its proper place. Essentially, God is promising to give us what we need. And not only do we have what we need but also we have joy in the process. The Father gives us Christ himself to be our confidence and our contentment. And with

71

the all-sufficient, all-powerful Christ taking care of our husband, family, and ministry, *what man can do* is an impotent, idle threat. "There is none like God, O Jeshurun, who rides through the heavens to your help, through the skies in his majesty" (Deut. 33:26). The role of helper to your husband is a joy-filled, God-enabled role that reminds you to keep looking to the heavens for your help as you emulate your Father.

The Husband of One Wife

Marriage between one man and one woman, although profusely debated in the public square in the West in recent days, has never been an assumption in the majority world or in the history of humanity. During a membership interview for our church, a man shared a perplexing story of how he had multiple marriage-type relationships with women in different countries. Now, as a Christian, he wanted to know which one was his wife and how to take care of the other children. An article in our newspaper announced an airline's new policy that "your fourth wife flies free" in honor of a ruler in a nearby country who had just married his fourth wife. When my husband traveled to a nearby country to minister there, he brought back this interesting anecdote. "Every pastor I met," he said, "introduced himself to me like this: 'My name is So-and-so; I have one wife and however-many kids.'" We thought it was so peculiar that a Christian man would mention that he specifically has one wife. Then one of our church members from that country explained to us that the rules of English grammar might be the reason the pastors said that they have "one" wife instead of "a" wife. Even so, in this half of the world, monogamous, state-recognized marriages are not assumed. Concubine-type relationships, girlfriends, and other female companions are acceptable in many places. I suppose it couldn't hurt for married pastors to affirm that they are, in fact, legally married to *only* one wife.

I realize that many of the women reading this book may not have married a pastor. Perhaps you married an orthodontist who was later called into pastoral ministry. Or you married a shopkeeper who was called to be a missionary. God is sovereign, and he may call any man he wills into pastoral ministry and equip that man to do his will. Besides the "only one wife if you're married" clause, 1 Timothy 3 and Titus 1 list nearly twenty requirements for a potential under-shepherd of the Lord's sheep. But where is the list of qualifications to be an elder's *wife*? Scripture-based ecclesiology offers no explicit job description for the office of pastor's wife because there is no such office.

From Empty Nesters to Nursing Moms

Even though there is not a formal office for the elder's or pastor's wife, some wives feel pressure to function as a coelder or an unpaid staff member of the church. Many women may see the needs of the church and even feel a desire or pressure to *act* with the authority of an elder or a pastor. Expectations of ministry wives all over the world are as diverse as the cultures and needs of the people. A pastoral search committee told a friend of mine that her gifts would be "a nice bonus" to her husband's potential ministry as their pastor. Other wives are asked in pastoral interviews, "So, what ministry will you lead if your husband is hired?" Another was told that the church would consider her an effective pastor's wife if she simply permitted him to do his job and "stayed out of his way." We need God's wisdom when navigating these various ideas regarding the role of the minister's wife. Direction in ministry can take on many forms. But for the sake of God's glory in the church, there is a specific ministry clearly worth a minister's wife's efforts, thoughtfulness, and prayers—a wife's ministry to her husband and family.

To state it negatively, a minister's wife should not be persuaded that ministry to her husband and family is nominal and diminishing when compared to other opportunities she has to serve in and through the church. A host of wonderful ministry opportunities is included in this category of subordinate ministries (which, for me, includes writing this book). Of course, a ministry wife desires to be "sold out for the kingdom" and to use her God-given gifts accordingly. She understands that the Lord has given her everything and that he is worthy of her everything. But she would be selling the wrong domain if she were to forgo her God-given responsibility of faithfully serving her husband and family because she has "better" things to do. None of us really wants to neglect or disown this main ministry that God has certainly handpicked for us. We want to be faithful to serve God through building up the body of Christ, starting with the needs we see right in front of us at the breakfast table.

A few years ago the subject of seasonal ministry was brought up around the lunch table where I sat with the other elders' wives in our church. Some of us are empty nesters or nearly empty nesters, while some of us have nursing babies at home. What is required of our husbands in their jobs greatly varies. These men also have various degrees of health and physical capacities to serve. Between the bowtie pasta and the panini, we marveled at how exceedingly difficult it would be if all of us elder's wives were called to the same area of formal service in our church. Our husbands need us in different ways. Our families are in different seasons of life. Our different children require different care. Our gifting and passions are all so *very* different, and we all serve in various capacities. But we share one ministry in common, which is ministry to our husbands—to be his one wife and helper with all the power of Christ, who so mightily works in us. There are so many needs where we could be serving, and we do serve! We marveled at how, in the midst of all the requests and pressures, there is but one man whom we are called to serve and serve alongside, and there is one God-man who serves us all.

How May I Help You?

Can an elder's wife learn anything from the other women in the church? Does the minister's wife need discipleship? Since the pastor's wife lives under the pastor's roof, is she beyond the need of shepherding from anyone else? We live out our answers to these questions each and every day. I would contend that just like every other church member, we need discipleship, intentional care for our soul, and direction in ministry. In fact, the ministry to our husband and children is so significant that we need help learning how to do it. We have a need to be trained in the area of loving our husband and children, as Paul directed Timothy in his leadership of the older women at this church in Titus 2:4: "Train the young women to love their husbands and children." The need for training and direction implies that loving our husband and children does not come as naturally as we might like to think. (Can I get an "Amen"?) We need the women in our church in order to be a healthy church member, wife, and mother.

Of course none of us would claim to be beyond needing this Titus 2 help. A woman sent me an e-mail the other day introducing herself as "a pastor's wife in training." Her fiancé was in seminary and was looking forward to taking his first pastorate a week after graduation and a month after their wedding. Sometimes we have little experience in life, marriage, and ministry before we are thrust into informal leadership roles simply by association with our husband.

Many of us are young. Some of us are newlyweds. Some of us are far away from home. *None* of us has finished the race marked out for us. We *all* have a need for endurance (Heb. 10:36).

You may not have envisioned being the wife of a minister, but God has planned to glorify himself in you, as you trust him for all things. He has lovingly planned good works for you to walk in (Eph. 2:10). Trust in the God who promises to be your help and your strength.

Instead of giving in to fear when we see that we are incapable and insufficient, we should see our weaknesses as opportunities to rely on the sufficiency of Christ. In our inadequacies, we look to God's provision as he directs us to seek out older women from whom we can learn how to love our husband and children. Jesus inspired Paul to write Titus 2, so we can trust that these instructions are for our good and his glory. This kind of humility and teachability influences the women in the church. "When I saw you praying with her [an older woman], I thought to myself, 'Why don't I ask an older woman to pray with me?'" a middle-aged woman in my church once told me. As for me, it isn't too difficult to see that I need help from other women. That much is obvious! I roll up to baptism services by myself with our four children in tow, all of whom want to take a dive into the swimming pool. It takes an average of three teenagers and other ladies to help me with my kids at some ministry events while my husband is otherwise occupied.

And even beyond the physical help that fellow church members are so eager to give, there are older women in my life who *regularly* text or call to ask how they can pray for us. Often they'll pray right there on the phone with me in the middle of my chaotic day. What a gift God has given to the church, that we have need for one another's help and prayers.

I've been blessed to see how the women in my church are instruments of God for my sanctification. My sinful heart busies itself manufacturing idols out of whatever supplies are available. For example, I have a love-hate relationship with comparing. I love to compare myself to other wives when it will make me look better. I hate to compare myself to other wives when it makes them look better. Such an ego is overinflated and prone to burst into a million shards of self-pity. As independent and self-sufficient as I would like to be, it has been a blessing to learn from other women. Their example models to me that a wife who draws on the strength and creative energy of God, "who richly provides us with everything to enjoy" (1 Tim. 6:17), will not lack anything she needs for ministry to her husband. That's how grace is esteemed as glorious. "Indeed, we are never soundly humbled till grace is glory in our esteem; that is, until it appears excellent and victorious."[10] Each family has unique needs that require specific help and support, and by God's grace he gives us everything we need to facilitate this help.

Because you are "one flesh" with your husband, you can consider your ministry to your husband as part of a joint effort with him in ministering to the body of Christ. It is not as though *you* (singular) each have a ministry, but that *you* (plural) have a ministry together. This thought revolutionized my perspective on ministry, and I pray it encourages you as well.

In the next two chapters I'll develop this idea further and wrap up some thoughts on ministry to an under-shepherd. "She does him good, and not harm, all the days of her life" (Prov. 31:12). After all, you're the only wife he's got!

5

Undergirding
the Overseer

In seminary an older pastor shared with our class, "Sometimes you're going to have to clean the bathroom." He was talking about pastoral ministry, but he wasn't referring to dealing with sin or counseling a person through something horrific. Pastoral ministry certainly involves those things, but he was talking about literal bathrooms with dirty toilets and sinks. Established churches with large staffs usually delegate a staff person to do the janitorial work that greatly blesses every human being present. Think about it—would you be eager to gather with God's people in a place where the bathroom was neglected? Not likely. The pastor was making a point that the overseers, among other things, oversee, in some way, everything. Including the bathroom sink.

It may go without saying that a distinction of pastoral

ministry is the work of shepherding. But perhaps this may not go without saying, because we, too, struggle with discerning pastoral ministry roles much like the early church did (Acts 6:1–6). The apostles faced an overwhelming service task by wisely delegating to other leaders among them called "deacons." "But we will devote ourselves to prayer and to the ministry of the word" (Acts 6:4), the twelve apostles decided. Ministry tasks get delegated as churches grow and mature, and sometimes the leaders may need to clean the bathrooms. Sure enough, in the early months of our church plant my husband ended up doing toilet paper ministry, checking the bathrooms before potluck gatherings to make sure everything was in order.

Toward the end of his life Paul listed out the suffering he had endured for the gospel and then he said, "And, apart from other things, there is the daily pressure on me of my anxiety for all the churches" (2 Cor. 11:28). The suffering, the priority of prayer and preaching, and "apart from other things," *the daily pressure*! As our minister-husbands "equip the saints for the work of ministry" (Eph. 4:12), we need to come alongside them and specifically support them in their specific calling. Lest we feel our dignity is diminished in our calling to be a helper, we need to recall that in ministering to our husband, we jointly minister to the church, which is a service unto the Lord. Across the globe we all face different challenges. What we have in common, though, is the author and perfecter of our faith, Jesus Christ. So how can a wife minister to her husband as he faces the daily pressure of anxiety for the church? I think one way we can learn to do this is to look at what God's Word says about the characteristics of the pastor and his tasks.

One place to start looking for specific ways to minister to our husbands is the list of elder/pastor qualifications in 1 Timothy 3 and Titus 1. Lest we think we should skip over these passages because they are directly applied to men, we ought to pause for consideration to gain a heart of wisdom. Because all Scripture is God-breathed and useful for our edification and encouragement, we can assume there is reproof and instruction for us to apply from these passages.

After we read that the potential elder/pastor (if he is married) must be "the husband of one wife" (1 Tim. 3:2; Titus 1:6), we see that if he aspires to this noble task, he must be of noble character. But what's unique about the combined list of nearly twenty character traits is that they are not actually unique. Take some time to look over these qualities and see for yourself. Are not these traits that *every* Christian man ought to aspire to by God's grace? But one quality is peculiar to the elder/pastor, and I'll elaborate more on that in a moment.

Manage His Own Household

We don't have space to discuss each and every one of the character traits, but there are a few that I'd like to highlight. One of the first things that stand out in this list is that an elder "must manage his own household well, with all dignity keeping his children submissive" (1 Tim. 3:4). This is a task charged to Christian men worldwide. It is globally applicable to all Christian husbands in all times and epochs. Leading your family well is something every Christian husband, from the Kenyan bush to the urban metropolis in the Arabian Peninsula to the suburban American Midwest, ought to aspire to. Households may look different across the world, but the task remains a biblical principle for Christian husbands everywhere to apply.

Yet perhaps at no time in the history of Christianity has this task been held to greater public derision than today. Even in Christian circles, the concept of the husband's headship over his home is sometimes met with skepticism. Ephesians 5:20–23 is often viewed as irrelevant to the modern family. The calling of Christian husbands to be the self-sacrificing head of their family is decapitated by the idea that there is no head in a marriage where men and women are equal. Yet God's Word remains true—the head of the wife is the husband, as Christ is the head of the church, *and* men and women are equal in personhood yet given different, complementary roles. God's Word alone gives us the category for understanding how both of those statements can be true at the same time.

How does a minister's wife see herself in light of this? How might she faithfully live in submission to her Creator, who designed her to submit to her husband's sacrificial and loving authority as unto Jesus? Households across the globe must be reordered by gospel grace in order to live as those who are citizens of a heavenly kingdom. In this sin-sick world, where even believers sin against one another, considering God's design for marriage is a task that is *only* for the faint of heart. It is *only* for the faint of heart because the proud will surely stumble over the humility it takes to seek God's help for marriage. We need the Spirit of wisdom and revelation in the knowledge of God to enlighten the eyes of our hearts so that we may know what is the hope to which he has called us, and what are the riches of his glorious inheritance in the saints, and what is the immeasurable greatness of his power toward those who believe (Eph. 1:17–19). When we understand just how faint our strength is, we can rely on God's grace to discern his call on our lives. Humble men and women feel their need for grace more acutely than the proud. May God grant us this humility.

We are not alone in our quest to live as God designed us. This hope, this inheritance of the kingdom, and this power are according to the work of God's great might that he worked in Christ when he raised him from the dead (v. 20). And this Christ whom we serve is not merely raised from the dead, but God seated him at his right hand in the heavenly places, far above all rule and authority and power and dominion, and above every name that is named, not only in this age but also in the one to come (v. 21). It is this

Christ who created us, and it is this Christ whom we serve. When we talk about "roles," we are not talking about roles in a play but a cosmic metanarrative woven to the praise of God's glory.

We must submit to Christ, who is Lord over all things— all things have been put under his feet, and he has been named head over all things to the church, which is his body, the fullness of him who fills all in all (vv. 22–23). To the praise of the glory of Christ, wives submit to their husbands as unto Christ. A wife's submission to her husband is not merely a picture of the church's submission to her head, Christ. Our obedient submission as unto Christ is in part fulfilling the plan of Christ to have his fullness fill all in all in his reign as king over the cosmos. This emanation of the gospel is no trifling or circumstantial outworking of cultural Christianity. It is not just some social construct devised to manage homes more practically (i.e., the buck has to stop *somewhere*). It is part of God's plan to glorify his Son in ways that we cannot even envision because we are finite and fallen. There is an invisible audience watching God's glory fill all things.

This must be the resounding grace that reverberates in the heart of a wife. Her marriage is not just a partnership for making life more bearable and less lonely. Her marriage is not just a means of procreation in a (currently) socially acceptable context. Her marriage is not just a means to personal fulfillment and collaborative financial or material gain. A wife's submission to Jesus in submitting to her husband is a victory banner she waves as Jesus advances his kingdom. The scorn of modernity is no match for the pleasure of God as we submit to husbands as they lead us, wash us with the Word, and daily die to themselves for us. Our glad-hearted submission to Jesus is a terror to all rule, authority, power, and dominion that would dare raise its ugly head in rebellion to the one true Head. "See how he loves us!" we say as we consider the cross he bore in our stead, and we gladly follow his lead.

Certainly an elder can "manage his own household well" with greater poise and confidence when his wife is supportive—supportive of him, of his leadership in their family, and of his leadership in the church. But above and beyond "supportive," a pastor's wife submits first to the loving rule of the risen King. In this regard, the minister's wife has a practical, direct, and strategic role in her husband's potential to shepherd the flock of God. Many women's Bible studies discuss how to become a Proverbs 31 woman. *An excellent wife, who can find!* These studies would also do well to caution women *against* becoming a Proverbs 21 woman:

> It is better to live in a corner of the housetop
>> than in a house shared with a quarrelsome
>>> wife. . . .
> It is better to live in a desert land
>> than with a quarrelsome and fretful woman.
>> (Prov. 21:9, 19)

I like to joke with my husband that when I am a quarrelsome and fretful woman, he is in *double* trouble. Our roof is less than habitable *and* we live in a scorching desert. Only the grace of God can keep a wife from becoming the common denominator of dissension in her home and to strive for unity and peace instead. Only the mercy shown to us at the cross can inspire us to build our home under the headship of our husband to the glory of Christ.

Able to Teach

The peculiar quality of an elder/pastor is that he must be "able to teach" (1 Tim. 3:2). It may be tempting to see yourself as helpless when it comes to assisting your husband in his teaching ability. Since we got married, I have certainly found myself wading around in the shallow gray area of, "Do I tell him this feedback on his sermon? Do I wait? How do I say it? Is critiquing that point helpful for our marriage?"

It's funny to us now, but I'll never forget the feeling of shame and horror as I realized that my husband's translator botched a sermon illustration about sin. In essence, via the translator, my husband told a congregation that their chicken dinner tasted like dog food. There were no rocks to hide under in the moment. Being subject to miscommunications like that early on in our ministry made it easier to be humble later. Years later at our church plant, my husband unknowingly said something in his sermon that offended all the Australians present, a phrase that is harmless in American English but crass and foul in the Australian dialect. Thankfully a few Aussies approached Dave after the service and discreetly warned him that he would do well to never say those words again from the pulpit. Dave was gladly forgiven for his blunder. "It's nothing, mate!" The church, Christ's multiethnic bride, is beautiful, and she is also gracious and accommodating.

Most ministers' wives don't have comprehensive knowledge of all cultures to give their husband feedback on how his words will be received. We may not have training in grammar to catch mistakes in sermons and lessons. We may not have read volumes of systematic theology to provide theological critique. We may not have time to sit in the basement every Sunday morning before dawn and listen to our husband practice his sermon (as one of my friends does). But we can support him in his grace-driven efforts *to be able to* teach the Word of God. Lest we give in to the temptation to be bored with sermonizing week-in and week-out, let's remember what preaching is.

Preach the Word

None of us can authoritatively conclude what God is doing in our lives. But we want to know, don't we? We crave a word from God to clarify what he would have us do or to comfort us because we don't know what he's doing. People in our churches and communities turn to those in ministry to hear about God's will and character. I've heard some people ask my husband, "Pastor, give us a new word from the Lord." They look disappointed when he points them to Scripture and says, "These words are thousands of years old, and the Bible still speaks today." We would jump at the chance to hear God speak to us, but we are so slow to open our Bible and believe that his written Word is sufficient to renew our minds so we can think rightly about what he's doing.

The heavens tell of the glory of God (Ps. 19:1–6), but the clouds can't talk about God's will, according to which the psalmist prays to be pardoned and sanctified. People in our churches and communities (indeed, *all* of us) need the Bible to reveal to us our blindness, helplessness, and guilt induced by sin. As inspiring as it may be, the majesty of a sunset does not tell us about the cross where the Son of God was crucified on our behalf. We need the Bible to tell us of God's remedies for our sin, the deadliest obstacle to our fellowship with him.

Do you crave personal, authoritative communication from God? It is revealed in his Word, the Bible. I have seen eyes misty with tears when women come to realize this for the first time. I recall a woman in Bible study holding a Malayalam translation of the Bible in her hands, and she said, "I can't believe it. He is *speaking*! To me. Through *this*." What mercy we have been shown—that the Creator who spoke us into existence would speak to us, his humble creation. Do we treasure his Word, believing that we can't live on bread alone? We get the gracious privilege of receiving nourishment from God's Word along with our sisters and brothers. Perhaps as a minister's wife you have the privilege of sitting under your husband's teaching as he carries out his call to announce God's powerful, wonder-working Word. Read Paul's words to Timothy regarding this task:

> I charge you in the presence of God and of Christ Jesus, who is to judge the living and the dead, and by his appearing and his kingdom: preach the word; be ready in season and out of season; reprove, rebuke, and exhort, with complete patience and teaching. (2 Tim. 4:1–2)

The heralding of God's Word does things in people's lives that we struggle to comprehend. The work of the Word is supernatural, cultivating fruit and inciting the praise of all of heaven. God ordains his Word to effectively do his bidding through preaching. Souls are raised from the dead, hearts are hardened, the saints are comforted, and sin is exposed (to name just a few effects). The preaching of God's Word is no mere information download; it's a feast for the soul.

When we think about the importance of God's Word, we can't help but think of *why* it is so important that God's people understand it:

> Pursue the pastoral metaphor a little further: Israel's sheep were reared, fed, tended, retrieved, healed and

restored—for sacrifice on the altar of God. This end of all pastoral work must never be forgotten—that its ultimate aim is to lead God's people to offer themselves up to him in total devotion of worship and service.[11]

The Word of God is the greatest comfort we have to offer at a funeral, the most powerful message we can give to someone in bondage, and the sharpest sword we can wield in battle with the Devil. "Able to teach" means that one is an approved workman who knows how to help other people understand the gravity of what God says to us in the Bible. No wonder the apostles felt such a sense of urgency to devote themselves to prayer and teaching God's Word. Like them, we affirm the importance of the pastor's preaching of the Word of God, praying for the Spirit of God to use their poor, lisping, stammering tongues to boldly preach the gospel.

Persevering with Preachers

Praise God that the burden of sustaining your husband's faith is not on you. God himself has sealed all believers with the Holy Spirit, who is a guarantee of our inheritance until we obtain it. He who began a good work in you and your husband will himself carry it on effectively to the praise of his glorious grace (Eph. 1:1–6).

That means you are free. Grace carries you along and frees you to be a cheerful helper to your husband. Grace empowers you to love—believing all things, hoping all things, and enduring all things. Grace also grounds you firmly in the bedrock of God's faithfulness and not in the changing times and seasons of ministry. By grace you can sit under your husband's preaching of the Word, knowing that God is magnified as he uses our fragile jars of clay to show his might. This ongoing trust in the Lord is cultivated in the heart as we steep ourselves in God's Word. When you read the Bible, do you recognize and tremble before the awesome majesty of God's speaking to you? When we read and study God's Word, we must expect that we can and will meet with God.

As you ask God to prepare your husband to preach each week, ask him to prepare your heart to listen. Something I personally struggle with is listening attentively during the sermon as my husband preaches, especially if I've heard it before. My husband paces back and forth in our room and in the bathroom, practicing his sermon the day before we gather for corporate worship. I also listen to my husband speak every day throughout the week.

It's easy to tune out, even if we don't mean to, when we're used to hearing someone's voice all the time. Pray for the grace you need to make intentional efforts to engage in the sermon while your husband is preaching. I love how the ladies in my church support my efforts to be a learner alongside them as they discuss the sermon with one another over lunch after the worship service.

As we read God's Word, we find many specific things we ought to pray for our elders and pastors, and they are apt fodder for your prayers for your husband. Prayer calls down supplies from heaven to do the Lord's work here on earth. John Piper has likened prayer to "a wartime walkie-talkie."[12] Although our husband's heading into a meeting at the office or going off on just a normal Tuesday morning may not seem as though he is going into the pit, we are reminded by God's Word that the battles are primarily spiritual. Pray that your husband would "share in suffering as a good soldier of Christ Jesus" (2 Tim. 2:3) and that he would avoid getting "entangled in civilian pursuits, since his aim is to please the one who enlisted him" (v. 4). In his efforts to serve with this single-minded devotion, pray that your husband would "remember Jesus Christ, risen from the dead, the offspring of David, as preached in my gospel, for which I am suffering, bound with chains as a criminal. But the word of God is not bound!" (vv. 8–9).

Paul says that his commitment to continue preaching the gospel in the face of intense suffering and pain is because there are brothers and sisters in the Lord who have not yet responded to the call of God in the gospel. "Therefore I endure everything for the sake of the elect, that they also may obtain the salvation that is in Christ Jesus with eternal glory" (v. 10). Why does your pastor-husband persevere in preaching the gospel even when it seems that nobody cares, or that people would rather hear something else, or when he suffers ridicule for it? There is a holy stubbornness that compels a minister to continue to announce the good news in the face of opposition. He preaches into the darkness because a brother or a sister may yet hear him and respond in faith and repentance. Our family is not yet all gathered into the fold. Take great comfort from Jesus's promise in John 10:16, "And I have other sheep that are not of this fold. I must bring them also, and they will listen to my voice. So there will be one flock, one shepherd." We do not preach the gospel in vain or into a void.

Even though soldiers suffer loss and endure hardship, it is with joyful and expectant hope that we pray for our husbands in their soldiering work for the gospel. Does that idea freak you out (even just a little)? In the middle of typing this section, I felt that I needed to find something to "nervous snack" on. Conflict caused by gospel preaching is scary, and it is real. Conflict caused by our sins, egos, emotions, and misunderstandings is also scary and real. If this reality makes you feel nervous for your husband's sake, your family's sake, or for your church's sake, then I would venture to say that this means you are human. Pain hurts. Enduring in conflict can be agonizing. Even so, we have a very real and near help in the Lord Jesus, who promised he would be with us even to the end of the age.

The promises of oversight and omnipresence that Jesus gave in his Great Commission are ours for the wholehearted believing (Matt. 28:18–20). If Jesus is with us to the end of the age and all authority has been given to him, then surely he is with us as we seek to support our pastor-husbands. And surely Christ receives praise as we toil and struggle with all of his energy, which so powerfully works in us.

6

So, You Married the Man Who Marries People

As wives of ministers we sometimes feel that we are uniquely challenged in our efforts to serve God, our husband and family, and the church. May I humbly submit to you that *every* woman probably feels this way? You are not alone. With that being said, may I also cheerfully encourage you that *Jesus knows* about your challenging circumstances and that *he loves you*?

One morning when our church was gathered for worship, I sat in the back of the room, with other moms holding tiny babies. After the worship service I was talking with a new mom who told me that she felt so defeated, having spent the morning taking care of her newborn daughter while trying to participate in the service. She said, "I wonder if the effort to get here was even worth it. This is just so hard!" I can totally sympathize with her feelings, and I told her so. Then out of the corner of my eye I noticed another woman standing off to the side and chatting with people. I knew that this sister also faces challenging circumstances in participating in corporate worship. She doesn't share her real name with people for security reasons; her life is in danger because of her loyalty to Jesus. Each time she gathers with other believers, she prays for protection for herself and others.

In our love-hate relationship with comparing ourselves to others, we are tempted to evaluate that scene with an air of contempt for the woman whose challenges seem comparatively trivial. But both women face *real* challenges, and both women receive *real* strength and grace from Jesus. When we are preoccupied with circumstances, we miss the real grace that is available to us. And there is nothing trivial about needing or receiving grace. As we recognize that we are all in this overarching circumstance of needing and receiving grace from Jesus, we see instead an opportunity to connect with other women and remind them of the grace we *all* need. In this light, we see that we, as ministry wives, are not aloof from the other women in our church. The different life seasons and circumstances that seem to unravel our potential for relationships with our sisters in Christ are actually occasions to see that we are all the same.

Airline passengers are instructed, in cases where oxygen masks are needed, to assist the helpless before putting on their own masks. In the same way, we need to experience God's grace before we can point others to it. In this chapter I hope to dig in to even more specific ways that grace carries us.

Well Thought of by Outsiders

White noise is constant, whether or not we consciously hear it. Our reputations are similar. In the context of the people around us, we live in our reputation and embody the assumptions that people make about us. You may think this is a good thing or a bad thing, but we must all at least acknowledge that it is a "thing." And this thing, I would argue, is something that God intends to leverage for his glory in the church. See the description of an elder that Jesus inspired Paul to write down in 1 Timothy 3:

> Moreover, he must be well thought of by outsiders, so that he may not fall into disgrace, into a snare of the devil. (1 Tim. 3:7)

I need to say from the outset that this joyful burden of having a good reputation among nonbelievers is something that Jesus is willing and able to carry for you. My aim right now is to show you that 1 Timothy 3:7 describes just another strategic way that God is glorified among the nations.

As a woman in a foreign country I face interesting social scenarios. No doubt, even while living in your home country, you face similar situations in which you aren't quite sure what to do or how to behave. For example, in this global city filled with men from different religious backgrounds and cultures, I am never certain how to greet them. Should I engage in small talk with the doorman of our building? Should I shake hands with the government official who helped me file some paperwork? Is it appropriate to make eye contact with men as I pass by them in the hallway, as I would naturally do in my home country? In this region of the world especially, people view women as *embedded* in the men who are their authority (whether father, brother, or husband), so they see my behavior as directly reflecting the character and integrity of my husband. I recall the instructions in Ephesians 4:10 to live in a manner worthy of the gospel. Even in just typing this, I can feel the weight of my responsibility to act honorably. How do grace and faith affect how I think about this?

As a wife of a minister, you know that eyes are watching you. A few may be looking for cause to malign, others are looking for an example to follow, and some are simply curious. The eyes of outsiders, as described in 1 Timothy 3:7, may be looking for all three. Because our reputations are like white noise, this elder qualification plays out in our daily lives, whether or not we realize it. And just like everything else in our lives, our reputation and our husband's reputation is something that we get to cheerfully entrust to the Lord. We don't fret or get anxious about anything but cast our burdens on him because he cares for us (1 Pet. 5:7). The same Jesus whose inspired Word says, "Walk in wisdom toward outsiders, making the best use of the time" (Col. 4:5), and "Look carefully then how you walk, not as unwise but as wise, making the best use of the time, because the days are evil" (Eph. 5:15–16), is the same Jesus who became to us wisdom: "And because of him you are in Christ Jesus, who became to us wisdom from God, righteousness and sanctification and redemption" (1 Cor. 1:30). We apprehend Christ's wisdom by faith through his powerful, sufficient Word. Is any one of us lacking wisdom? Let her ask God, who gives generously to all without reproach, and it will be given to her (James 1:5). God is able to help us! "To this end we always pray for you, *that our God may make you worthy of his calling* and may fulfill every resolve for good and every work of faith by his power" (2 Thess. 1:11).

The wisdom we need to live upright lives comes freely from Christ, who has given us his Word. The breath of God breathed out Scripture, and his Word is what brings us strength and peace and equips us for service (1 Tim. 3:16). Are you tempted to focus on being your own public relations manager? The Word of God beckons us to stay laser-focused on who *God* is and what he has done. In God's Word we read that his glory is of primary import. So with glad hearts, by his grace, we let his Word dwell in us richly (Col. 3:16). And his provision of wisdom erupts in our hearts in thankfulness to God.

Hospitable

Is there another elder qualification more intimidating to a wife than this one? "Therefore an overseer must be . . . hospitable" (1 Tim. 3:2). In the region of the world where I live, it is not uncommon for everyone—men, women, and children alike—to address any woman as "Mum." Whether or not she has children, a woman is seen in this nurturing role in all her relationships. I'll never forget my surprise years ago when I opened the side door of our home to see the landlord's maintenance crew seated on the steps, resting in the shade after a morning of work. One of the men stood up and said, "Mum, it's time for our lunch." I quickly sent someone to the closest sandwich shop to pick up a hot lunch for the men. You can imagine the implications of a hospitable home as "nurturing and equipping" versus "entertaining and showing off."

On another occasion a neighbor walked into my kitchen and noticed my clean and empty kitchen sink. She pointed to the sink and asked, "No dishes?" I was so proud of myself that I said with flourish, "Yes!" I was so proud that she noticed. Her brow furrowed, "What? Why are you not feeding your family?" The implications of an empty sink in her mind meant that I was not serving the people who are dependent upon me for food. What a fascinating window into our expectations of ourselves as those who provide hospitality! The honor of extending hospitality is given to those who give. Since hospitality is a giving issue, it makes sense that our selfishness is what gets in the way of our hospitality. So, how do we avoid the roadblock of selfishness in our efforts to be hospitable? We look to Christ. Consider the principles laid out in 2 Corinthians 9:6–9 regarding the manner in which we ought to give:

> Whoever sows sparingly will also reap sparingly, and whoever sows bountifully will also reap bountifully. Each one must give as he has decided in his heart, not reluctantly or under compulsion, for God loves a cheerful giver. And God is able to make all grace abound to you, so that having all sufficiency in all things at all times, you may abound in every good work. As it is written, "He has distributed freely, he has given to the poor; his righteousness endures forever."

Jesus sows bountifully, and he will also reap bountifully. He is the one who decided in his heart to give his own life, and he did so neither reluctantly nor under compulsion. For the joy set before him he endured the cross for us (Heb. 12:2). Christ is *the* cheerful giver. He gives to the poor, and his righteousness endures forever. The same Jesus who purchased our lives from death and sin is able to make all grace abound to us. If Christ is our sufficiency in all things at all times, can there be *anything* he can't enable us to give freely to others in his name? The good works he has prepared from before time for us to walk in are there for the walking (Eph. 2:10). And we will walk in them by faith—

from the church's kitchen to the guest room to the sidewalk outside our house and even to our pocketbook.

Jesus gladly came "not to be served but to serve, and to give his life as a ransom for many" (Mark 10:45). He gave his life two thousand years ago, and he still gives his life every day as we live and move in him. He gives, *oh how he gives*! We do not regret that we are servants in hospitality to others, because we have first been served by Christ, and fellowship with him is worth everything. With Christ at the center of our motive and goal for hospitality, the gravitational pull to worship Christ alone pulls us away from distortions of hospitality that are really narcissistic service. Jesus, who gave his own life in the ultimate act of hospitality to bring us to his Father's house, is our provision for all our hospitality. We rejoice that the record of cheerful giving we want to have has already been credited to us by faith; we enjoy the freedom of fellowship with God via the righteousness of Christ. Are you lacking resources or cheerfulness to extend hospitality alongside your husband? Ask God, who freely gives and gives and *gives* to the praise of his glory.

Created to Be a Conduit of Grace

I am aware that all these exhortations toward service may sound like a clanging gong when you are struggling to simply love your husband. The various life seasons, struggles, and sticky situations represented in the women reading these pages are as diverse as we are. We don't hesitate to affirm that Jesus is sufficient still. In our appraisal of Christ's all-sufficient grace for us to love our husbands, we must acknowledge the root of our problems—our sin. If the most powerful influence in your life is Christ, being saved by God's glorious gospel, then why is it so hard to selflessly serve your husband (or anyone, for that matter)? Loving your God-fearing husband is hard because you married a man who is just like you—a sinner in need of God's grace.

Because of the cross, the problem of our sin has been solved. God in his holy wrath is not against us anymore because we are hidden in Christ. Reconciled to God vertically through Jesus, we are also reconciled to one another horizontally through Jesus. Everyone who belongs to God through Christ belongs to everyone else who belongs to God. We are not against each other anymore, as our first parents were at the outset of the fall in the garden of Eden. We are for each other's good, and the grace of Jesus is the only power on earth that can initiate, sustain, and preserve this kind of love to the end. Grace joined you into one flesh with your husband, so it must be by grace that we act accordingly. And what God has joined together, let no man separate (Matt. 19:6).

PART 3

Loving the
Bride of Christ

7

What on Earth
Is the Church?

We know that the church is a *people*, built together in an architecture designed and sustained by God, but sometimes we need to be reminded of that. One afternoon while driving through the United States on a visit, I got to see this idea in a living illustration via my third-culture kids.

"Mom, Dad! Look out the window! Quick!" our young daughter shouted from the backseat of the van. "You're not going to believe it. Look there! They have a Chili's restaurant in America also!"

After our guts stopped hurting from laughing so hard, my husband and I took turns trying to explain to the kids the concept of a franchise. "So, honey, it's the same restaurant with the same food, but in different places," I summarized for her as we pulled into the parking lot of the church building where we had an appointment that morning.

"Oh," she thought out loud, "so it's like church."

"Um," was my articulate answer.

"Where are we? Where's the church?" our son asked as he jumped from the van onto the parking lot.

"We're at the church, buddy."

Our family walked into the quiet church building on a weekday morning. Hardly anyone was around. The cafe in the atrium was dark, and chairs were on top of the tables. The bookstore was dark, and the glass door was closed. Entire hallways were dark as we made our way to the administrative part of the building. In a hushed whisper our young boy said, "This shopping mall is closed." It took me a moment to understand what he meant, and then it hit me. Both conversations from the past hour had to do with our children's perspective. Of course my daughter was surprised to see "her" local restaurant in another country. Of course my son thought the church building was a shopping mall, because our church gathers in the ballroom of a hotel attached to a shopping mall. Every week he walks past a bustling food court and crowded stores to where we gather for corporate worship.

Just like these childlike responses to the world around them, we need to cultivate a childlike faith in response to what God's Word says about the nature of the church. I'm convinced that a robust ecclesiology not only will help remind wives of ministers of why we're here but will also propel us toward thoughtful engagement in our joint ministry with our husband. Under that premise I want to spend this chapter and the few that follow talking about what the church is and the supernatural nature of her existence, ministry, and goal.

Rooted in Eternity

A church is a *people*—something that could be assumed, but we dare not assume it. If we want to be faithful to the precise definition of *church* in God's Word, in English grammar we should say that *we are* the church. All the sheep who belong to Christ belong to his body, and this mysterious reality transcends all earthly realities. Speaking of the church, C. S. Lewis said in his satirical *Screwtape Letters*, "I do not mean the Church as we see her spread but through all time and space and rooted in eternity, terrible as an army with banners."[13] The church is not a club, an organization, or a nonprofit entity. The church is not just about a Sunday morning worship service. The church is a gathered people who exist by God's grace to display the glory of Jesus and testify to his goodness as he is about his work of bringing all God's prodigals home.

We see in the New Testament the humbling brilliance of God's grace to the church in that the entire covenant community of God is actually the spiritual temple in which he chooses to dwell. We are adopted into God's family, and Jesus has gone to prepare a place for us in his Father's house—*yes*. And we are still here, caught up in the already–not yet of God's kingdom, indwelled by the Holy Spirit while we grow up in every way into him who is the head, into Christ (Eph. 4:15). We cannot comprehend the love of God in Christ toward us by ourselves, for the architect has not designed his dwelling place in that way. We are members of one another, the community temple of priests in which God's presence delights to dwell:

> Do you not know that you are God's temple and that God's Spirit dwells in you? If anyone destroys God's temple, God will destroy him. For God's temple is holy, and you are that temple. (1 Cor. 3:16–17)

> Or do you not know that your body is a temple of the Holy Spirit within you, whom you have from God? You are not your own, for you were bought with a price. So glorify God in your body. (1 Cor. 6:19–20)

> Christ Jesus himself being the cornerstone, in whom the whole structure, being joined together, grows into a holy temple in the Lord. In him you also are being built together into a dwelling place for God by the Spirit. (Eph. 2:20–22)

> You yourselves like living stones are being built up as a spiritual house, to be a holy priesthood, to offer spiritual sacrifices acceptable to God through Jesus Christ. For it stands in Scripture: "Behold, I am laying in Zion a stone, a cornerstone chosen and precious, and whoever believes in him will not be put to shame." (1 Pet. 2:5–6)

God calls us to be a holy priesthood. We receive God's blessing and the yes to all his promises (that is, the person of Jesus), and we in turn become a blessing to others when we share his good news. To be a member of God's called-out people is not a matter of preference or taste but one of necessity. We are called "members" because we are members of a body. Being part of the church is not merely in reference to your taking up a seat on a Sunday morning at a worship service. It is more ontological than standing, sitting, and singing with others—we *are* members of one another.

> For as in one body we have many members, and the members do not all have the same function, so we, though many, are one body in Christ, and individually members one of another. (Rom. 12:4–5)

I don't mean to be gruesome here, but the biblical illustration of the church as a body really does beg this question: If you were to see a severed toe, wouldn't you look around to see *to whom* it belonged? So then, a Christian apart from a visible, gathered body of believers is a Christian *apart* from a visible, gathered body of believers. To be like living stones built up as a spiritual house is no trite thing. The church—God's people—indwelled and sealed by the Holy Spirit himself is an incomprehensible, spiritual-literal reality. It is a prophetic hope that whispers of the end when the dwelling place of God is forever among men.[14]

> I will make a covenant of peace with them. It shall be
> an everlasting covenant with them. And I will set them
> in their land and multiply them, and will set my sanc-
> tuary in their midst forevermore. My dwelling place
> shall be with them, and I will be their God, and they
> shall be my people. Then the nations will know that I
> am the LORD who sanctifies Israel, when my sanctuary
> is in their midst forevermore. (Ezek. 37:26–28)

Can we speak too highly of the utter brilliance of God's
design to shepherd his flock that he created with a need to
be gathered, fed, and led *together*? I love how Mark Dever
punctuates the importance of our understanding of ecclesiology: "The doctrine of the church is of the utmost importance. It is the most visible part of Christian theology, and it
is vitally connected to every other part."[15]

Body-Building Ministry

This is all just a glimpse into our awe-full privilege of helping our husbands in ministry, as we are fellow sheep serving the flock of God. In Ephesians 4 we read that when
Jesus ascended and led a host of captives, he gave gifts to
the church. This passage sheds light on Jesus's goals in giving different kinds of servant leaders to his church:

> He gave the apostles, the prophets, the evangelists,
> the shepherds and teachers, to equip the saints for the
> work of ministry, for building up the body of Christ,

until we all attain to the unity of the faith and of the
knowledge of the Son of God, to mature manhood, to
the measure of the stature of the fullness of Christ.
(Eph. 4:11–13)

On days when my husband's work in pastoring or my
role in helping him does not seem very meaningful, I remember Christ's explicit goals for his church. Those goals
are why we are still here and not in heaven. The privilege
of participating in Christ's fullness, filling all in all as more
and more people across the globe worship him as the one
true God, is why you are *here*. This is true whether you are
in Iowa City, Bangalore, Abu Dhabi, or Juarez. Even on a
mundane Monday morning our hearts can be thrilled with
the prospect that included among the gifts Jesus gave to
his church are your pastor-husband to serve and you to
help him serve—for the building up of his body. It throws
everything into perspective of the big picture when we remember that Jesus ordained that this body building has a
massive, Christ-centered goal: that the church would attain
to the unity of the faith and of the knowledge of him, to
mature manhood, and to the measure of the stature of his
fullness.

Christ is our Great High Priest (Heb. 4:14; 9:11), and
through him God makes us all into priests in a holy priesthood. He is also the means by which we are able to offer
spiritual sacrifices acceptable to God (1 Pet. 2:5). It is no
trivial thing or ethereal idea to consider that because of

Christ's sacrificial, atoning work on our behalf, we are able to enter the Most Holy Place. Serious consideration of the doctrine of ecclesiology shows us that *church* is not about us, as though we are the epoch of God's creative and redemptive purposes. Ecclesiology teaches that God's glory in his Son is local and tangible and real in our life and in the life of our church body, but it is also expansive and effusive and fills all in all. There is an eschatological arc, a forward-bending orientation of our ministry that we must keep in mind.

> In the new creation, all of God's people living throughout the new world will be high priests always in the presence of God because the dimensions of the heavenly holy of holies and God's ruling presence, symbolized by his throne, have broken in and expanded to include the entire new cosmos.[16]

Deep consideration of these things causes us to feel how the gravity of God's goal to glorify his Son through the church pulls on our perspective of just another Sunday, just another small group, or just another *anything* into a worshipful, joyfully serious place.

United Nations Worshiping the Risen Christ

It was planned weeks in advance, but for some reason it slipped my mind that my husband was going to preach at a new church plant in our country. Something my husband had said offhandedly a few days before that Friday reminded me. His preaching at that church plant meant that we would get up extra early, and I would drive us into a city that is known for less than favorable traffic conditions. On remembrance of that ministry opportunity my mind immediately went not to the incredible privilege of seeing a new church plant but to the traffic.

I groaned, "Ugh. What time do you think we're going to have to leave here?"

Unfazed by my grumbling, my husband cheerfully guessed that an hour would give us plenty of time to drive plus some extra time for getting lost (one must budget for getting lost here). I did the mental calculation of what time I would have to wake up in order to get all four kids ready to go at that hour, and I already felt weary.

That early morning did come, and, rising at dawn, I shuffled into our kitchen and made a beeline for the coffeepot. Out the kitchen window I noticed the sun, which had risen that morning, just like it does every morning. As I waited for the coffeepot to start doing its job, I stood in the corner where I could see a sliver of our city out the window. As the sun was rising over our city I remembered that in those buildings and on those streets were people yet walking in darkness. From down the hall I could hear that my husband was awake and going over his sermon in his usual manner, praying as he paced the floor and pacing the floor as he prayed. Humbled, my grumpy demeanor had a reality check. I thanked the Lord for the extravagant mercy I knew he was giving to me in that moment.

The drive into that city was every bit as stressful as I had imagined. We parked in a congested neighborhood and walked on dusty sidewalks, dodging cars that narrowly missed driving atop our children's little feet as we walked to the building where the church was gathered. The morning sun was already blazing by that time, and we could feel the dust find places to settle on our clothes and sweaty skin. We were not the only people walking in that crowd though. Like a rainbow of people, men and women from many nations found their way to various meeting spaces and buildings on that compound. Some of them were going to places where Christ is named as an aside, their good works taking front and center. Others would hear good news preached—on the cross, Jesus Christ has done for us what we could never do for ourselves, so throw yourself on him and accept the free grace of God. Nations were gathering together to worship Jesus, a fractional sliver of what we will see when men, women, and children from every tribe gather around the throne of God to worship the Lamb, who was slain for us. We found our way to the building where the church plant was gathered and were welcomed into the refreshing air-conditioning and fellowship with the saints.

What the Parking-Lot Ministry People See

We need to have our eternal perspective reminded all the time. Who and what is the church? Why does the church exist? The answers to these questions cast anchors on Christ that steady our hearts when we're discouraged and distracted. The fact that the church is a people created, called out, and gathered by God helps us in this regard. Have you heard the children's song in Sunday school: "Father Abraham Had Many Sons"? The song points back to Genesis 12:1–3, when God called Abraham out of idolatry and into worship of the one true God. Yahweh promised that Abraham would be the father of a great nation through whom the whole world would be blessed. God called him to have faith in him and his promise of future grace. We, like Abraham, are called to believe God, and our belief in God affects the way we live. Abraham trusted God and left his country, heading to a land that God promised to show him. He had never seen the Promised Land, but Abraham believed God would faithfully deliver him there, so he moved.

Like Abraham, we know that here we have no lasting city, but together we are seeking the city that is to come (Heb. 13:14). One day the nations will stream into the permanent city in the new heavens and the new earth, which is lit by the glory of God and the Lamb (Rev. 21:22–26). If your church has a parking-lot ministry or a greeting team, they get to see a shadow of this every week as God's people physically come together as a gathered people. Indeed, we

117

all get to enjoy the privilege of being part of a gathered people. Through this lens, see that Hebrews 10:24–25 has both immediate and eschatological relevance in our lives:

> Let us consider how to stir up one another to love and good works, not neglecting to meet together, as is the habit of some, but encouraging one another, and all the more as you see the Day drawing near.

Seeing myself in the big picture as part of the body of Christ (and the body of Christ in the big picture of God's plan to glorify his Son) has changed even the way I see my mundane task of helping get my family ready to go to meet with the church each week. How else does this change your perspective about being part of the bride of Christ?

In the next chapter we will turn to the task mentioned in Hebrews 10:24–25 of considering how to stir up one another to love and good works.

8

Gifted to Give
What God Has Given

I can't think of a single joy that out-joys our grace-enabled ability to worship God. He allows, commands, invites, instructs, and enables us to worship him and give him the glory that he deserves. In our happy worship of God we recognize that we haven't given him more glory than he had at the first, as though we add to him, but, rather, we receive (always receiving!) from him as we recognize that he is indeed all-glorious.

One of the unique ways that we are allowed to worship our Creator is by our service to him. We can't help but shake our heads in wonder at the fact that we are told to consider how we might encourage one another in the Lord.

And let us consider how to stir up one another to love and good works, not neglecting to meet together, as is the habit of some, but encouraging one another, and all the more as you see the Day drawing near. (Heb. 10:24–25)

We are created—finite and helpless without God—yet he enjoins us to strengthen one another. It *must* be that we do this through him, for there is no other way. We've seen that being a member of Christ's body, the church, is a defining aspect of who we are. Lest we adopt an overinflated or a diminutive view of who we were saved to be, the Bible describes a believer as a brick in a building, a sheep in a flock, a priest in a priesthood, and a member of a family and of Christ's body. Remembering the context of our faith as part of a community and a cloud of witnesses does a number on our prideful independence, doesn't it?

You probably already have an idea of what your role in service to the church ought to be. Other people, including those outside the church, may also be happy to categorize you as well. I was eating lunch with a group of friends from the community, a group of women with whom I'd been hoping to build deeper friendships, as we already had a similar passion for a unique community service. The ladies were telling stories of how they had met their significant other(s) and what kind of employment had brought them to this country. To the woman, each of them had met their man (or men) in a bar or a nightclub, and their goal in working in this country was evaluated by the size of his salary. Some stories were punctuated with accounts of one-night stands that developed into semi-exclusive relationships with one or more men, and the stories all included how much money the men made. When it was my turn to share about my husband, Dave, I blurted out, "We met at church. He's a pastor." A few ladies giggled, and one sneered, "Now we're all being judged," and the rest stared at their smartphone or their plate. I wondered how I could have avoided this awkward scene and what I could have said differently, and I even began to regret that I had accepted the invitation.

But later, when the group was otherwise engaged in ordering dessert, one woman tapped me on the shoulder and asked if she could talk with me. I pushed my chair out at an angle so I could speak with her, and I saw that her face was flushed. "My marriage is a mess," she whispered. Then she asked me what God had to say about her situation. Friends, being the wife of a minister may come with some baggage that the culture kicks aside as annoying, but to others in whom the Spirit of God is working, your ministry and presence in their life is what they have been hoping for when the world and their idols fail them. We dare not minimize the opportunity we have to serve others in and outside the body of Christ, even as we may feel preoccupied with helping to equip our husbands for their public ministry. "We need to remember that each ministry is unique and each marriage is unique, and God has uniquely gifted us for the position and role we are in."[17]

Grace for Our Giver's Remorse

Have you ever taken a young child shopping for a gift to give to someone else? Perhaps your child has been invited to a birthday party, or your children exchange gifts with each other and their cousins at Christmastime. On the shopping trip they pore over the things on display, take their sweet time making the right decision, and wrap the present with enthusiasm. But then giver's remorse kicks in, and they don't want to give the gift away.

Even as adults, we are not immune to giver's remorse when it comes to serving others. Some of us might regret that we have been gifted in a particular way, and are reluctant to serve using our gifts. Some of us look at another woman's gifts with envy. Some of us wonder why God won't allow us the same opportunities (or better ones, in our opinion) than what we see he has given other women. This kind of rivalry regarding our gifting isn't pretty, is it? When we experience this kind of regret, we do well to remember that God never experiences giver's remorse over the way he has gifted us as individuals and as a corporate body. We must remember that the gifts he gives are for a corporate reason, expression, and usefulness, since we are a people, the body, Christ's bride. And since he has gifted the church of which you are a member, there's no way in Christ that you are lacking.

We know that God has given us gifts, and we want to be good stewards of them, both for our personal lives and for the sake of the church. We want to have God's kingdom priorities in mind when we serve. We see needs all around us—so many needs! We are also creative. In fact, we are so creative that we know deep down that we could be serving more creatively, which is a good thing! We've been given desires to serve and love him and others well. We need God's grace to steward our gifts and opportunities well. The needs around us can potentially become soapboxes we stand on to rail against those who don't see the needs. We might struggle to serve, doing so with a low-grade sense of guilt that we aren't "doing enough for God's kingdom" or "dreaming big enough" in a manner worthy of God's grandeur. Do you see that even in using the gifts God has given us, *we need the grace of God that he freely gives*? Good stewardship starts and ends with a biblical perspective on our gifts (individually and corporately) and on the giver of those gifts.

How and Why Do We Serve?

I've found my perspective on gifting is helpfully recalibrated by considering the truths in a short passage in 1 Peter. It's not a "typical" passage on gifting that one might read in a spiritual gifts inventory or hear in a discussion on spiritual gifts. I do wish this passage was included in more "gift finding" resources, because it talks about the why and the how. *Why* did God gift us? *How* should we use our gifts?

As each has received a gift, use it to serve one another, as good stewards of God's varied grace: whoever speaks, as one who speaks oracles of God; whoever serves, as one who serves by the strength that God supplies—in order that in everything God may be glorified through Jesus Christ. To him belong glory and dominion forever and ever. Amen. (1 Pet. 4:10–11)

We could make many observations about this text on gifts. The first thing that stands out is that gifts are something we have received. Gifts are deliberately chosen by God and given by God, and our part is to receive. This idea in itself inspires enough courage to stop looking sideways at the gifts of other women. Their gifts were not chosen by them any more than your gifts were chosen by you. Regretting gifts, comparing gifts, and belittling gifts are an insult to the one who has given them. When we receive a gift from God, the proper response is to do what our momma taught us and say, "Thank you!"

A second, brief observation we can make from this passage is what happens to the gift after it is received. We use it to serve one another. The gift doesn't go in the pile of wrapping paper at the base of the Christmas tree to be fished out when we want to play with it. The gift goes to work. I hope I never forget the look on my daughter's face when she found that with her newly discovered reading skills, she could read the verses in my big adult Bible. Her eyes grew wide with wonder as she read Genesis 1:26. She read, "Then God said, 'Let us make man in our im . . . im . . .' Mommy? What does i-m-a-g-e say?"

"Image."

"Oh. Image. Then God said, 'Let us make man in our image.' In our image! I know this! God made us in his image! I'm reading it—the Bible—I'm *reading* it! Hey guys, listen . . ."

And my young reader trailed her little siblings around the apartment reading to them from the Bible as she was able to pick out the words. Gifts are made to go to work and bless others, and in using her God-given ability to read words, she was blessed.

The third observation I want to mention is the *how*. In a sense, we use our gifts with all our might, but ultimately we use our gifts with all of God's might by "the strength that God supplies." It is God who is working in us.

> God is able to make all grace abound to you, so that having all sufficiency in all things at all times, you may abound in every good work. (2 Cor. 9:8)

> For this I toil, struggling with all his energy that he powerfully works within me. (Col. 1:29)

> By the grace of God I am what I am, and his grace toward me was not in vain. On the contrary, I worked harder than any of them, though it was not I, but the grace of God that is with me. (1 Cor. 15:10)

The last observation I want to point out from 1 Peter 4:10–11 is the *why*. We receive gifts from God and use them to serve "in order that in everything God may be glorified through Jesus Christ." Honest service gives credit where it is due. Gifts are given by God and empowered by God to glorify God. However thrilling it is to receive a gift from God, and however much we love what we are able to do through God's strength, we would be remiss to glory in the gift. Being gifted and using gifts to bless others is ultimately not about us. The Spirit gave us gifts according to his will (Heb. 2:4) so that we might serve others in Jesus's name through God's strength. Our self-oriented ideas of gifting and calling are seen in a new light when we consider how the triune Godhead is working to display God's glory in the cosmos. "To him belong glory and dominion forever and ever. Amen" (1 Pet. 4:11b).

No Gifts Left Behind

Our ministry as women happens in so many diverse ways. The mind boggles with all the different contexts in which women around the world are raising up disciples. I recall hearing a friend of mine who is extraordinarily gifted in leadership say that when her children were young, she felt she was forced to push her leadership gift to the side. She did this with the hopes that she could pick it up later, when her children were grown, but in the meantime her gift was sitting idle, languishing in dystrophy. My reaction was to wonder at the possibilities of what I could do if only I had one fraction of her leadership gifts to lead my children better and reach my neighbors. I began to daydream about the way I could shepherd my young kids—communicate my expectations, vision cast for the weekend plans, direct them in decision making, and guide them through what was ahead. How might I manage my home better so that I could have a greater capacity of leading more people around me including the women in my apartment building whom I longed to reach? Leadership is most definitely a useful and necessary gift for mothers with young children.

No gifts are left behind, according to God's redemptive purpose in our lives, and his sovereign hand orders all things to his pleasure. I have no right to regret how God made me, but I have every reason to humbly submit to him and look to his hand with the happy expectation that he will give me things to do that he wants me to do and a way to do them so that he gets the glory.

We have no regrets or giver's remorse when we understand our God-giftedness and ministry opportunities in this light. Instead, we experience the simple joy of having been given something to share with others. We humbly thank the Lord that our husbands have been gifted for service. We look around at the Christian women in our lives and rejoice with them too. We are nothing but humble, grateful receivers of grace. None of this—no ministry, no gift, no act of service—is unto us. All our zeal and passion must find culmination in praise to God, the giver of all good gifts.

Whom should we serve? Where should we use our God-given gifts? Does God's Word give us direction? Or do we follow our heart? Or both? Is my husband my main ministry? What about my children? Or my home? Or my church? Or my next-door neighbor? Or . . . ? The quandary in these questions is almost tangible. We want to serve, we want to bless, and we want to do it right. One of the oft-asked questions I hear from women regarding using their gifts is where and how to spend their limited energy and time. Because God is wise and loving and will assuredly receive praise, the beginning of the answer to these questions is always another glad-hearted question. Look beside you and see. *Who has God given you to serve?*

Every Christian Woman's Privilege

The minister's wife is like all other wives in this regard: we are privileged to help our husbands, serve our family, love the church, and practice all the *one anothers* with the people around us by God's grace. We are all called—we are called to love, respect, and obey our husbands as they lead with servant-leader, Christlike humility. If we have children, we are called to love them and make a home for them. We are called to love the lost, make disciples, and serve the suffering. There is no need for this to be a soul-shrinking idea.

With restful assurance that we are doing what we ought to do, we can happily and humbly recognize that there are seasons of life (some short and some all encompassing) and that God's ways are above our human understanding of stewardship and gifting.

In Christ's subversive kingdom we understand that even giving cups of water in Jesus's name is service unto him. Small tasks cannot be demeaned as mere stepping-stones toward being asked to do something great someday. God is pleased as we do *all* things to his glory. It is no trifle that the Holy One is pleased with his children, and his joy is so effusive that Jesus said that he wants his joy to fill us: "These things I have spoken to you, that my joy may be in you, and that your joy may be full" (John 15:11).

As women who are citizens of the kingdom of heaven, we understand that being gifted by God is not an end in itself. We seek first Christ's kingdom, leveraging our situations and all our God-given, unique abilities for making much of Jesus in this world, which is so quickly passing away. In the overall scope of the letter to Titus and the Great Commission, the directive for women in Titus 2:3–5 "accords with sound doctrine" (v. 1). This doctrine must be passed from one generation to the next (Deut. 6:1–9; Pss. 145:4; 78:1–7). Discipleship is timeless until time runs out.

As daughters of the King, we dream global dreams for our family with eternity in mind, pursuing the good work of discipleship that will advance God's kingdom, using the gifts he has given us in the places he has planted us, prioritizing the people he has put in our lives.

This is true even if the race marked out before you in this season includes umpteen laps between the kids' room and your bed every night. We can gladly accept all the gifts, opportunities, weaknesses, and circumstances as from the Lord's hand, trusting that he is the one who will reveal their true worth in the last day. Whatever we've been given, we can accept as we look down the corridor of time and imagine generations of image bearers worshiping the King. Church leaders can also provide humble oversight and equip and affirm female disciple makers to use their gifts, even the gifts that take root in the home but may bloom outside of those four walls into the community and the world.

In this next and final chapter on learning to love the bride of Christ, we'll look at strength-and-weakness finders.

9

Weakness Finders and Christ's Sufficient Strength for Service

"How do you do it?" This is a question that nearly every woman has been asked or has asked another woman. One time I asked a new friend this question while I was seated at breakfast, trying to spear strawberries with a fork with one hand and cradling my fourth baby in the crook of my other arm.

"I know everyone must ask you this, but . . . ," I began.

". . . how do I do it?" She finished my question. I dug in for answers from my new friend. "Yes! Tell me how. I mean, I feel like I'm barely surviving. I can't even imagine your life. There's the kids, ministry, marriage, and showering. Do you even get to shower anymore?"

I figured she was a prime candidate to answer my burning *how* question because she was the mother of nine children, pregnant with her tenth, and married to a busy minister. They were traveling through our city as they investigated ministries in our region of the world, and I knew I had a brief window in which to get *the* holy-grail answer I had been looking for

My newborn squirmed in my arms for effect as I leaned in to hear my new friend's wise words. "We both live and serve by God's grace. God gives you grace for what he's given *you* to do. I look at your life, and *I* can't even imagine. God is the one who gives."

It was as if the wise King Solomon was sitting at my dining table. I was astonished at how profoundly true her words were. God is the giver of not only the gifts we use to serve but also the service opportunities themselves. Those are wise words from a woman who has been there (and remains in the middle of it). Grace turns our obsession with our abilities into a God-centered vision for ministry in which we see that "from him and through him and to him are all things. To him be glory forever. Amen" (Rom. 11:36). We look to God for direction and strength in serving his church: "For who sees anything different in you? What do you have that you did not receive? If then you received it, why do you boast as if you did not receive it?" (1 Cor. 4:7).

A Vision for Christ-Centered Service

The most important thing to know about my friend's wisdom is that she points to the question underneath the *how* question. The bigger question we need to ask when we think about how we are to serve the church and use our gifts is, *Who?*

When it comes to serving God as part of his church, a body of people in which "no one seek[s] his own good, but the good of his neighbor" (1 Cor. 10:24), we need to think first and foremost about God himself. God is the one who equips for service, provides opportunities to exercise our gifts, and establishes himself as the source and goal for our work. How does a ministry wife participate in this kind of community? We do it in view of who God is. We serve *unto the Lord* in the same manner in which other members participate: by grace through faith, walking in the good works God has prepared for us (Eph. 2:8–10).

We serve as a glad witness of the gospel to our neighbors because we rest in God's sovereign grace in salvation (Acts 13:48). There is urgency and blood-earnest seriousness in our ministry because we understand that God's just wrath against us in our sin is *the* gravest threat, and hell is horrific and real (Matt. 25:46; John 3:36). Our pleading witness is carried along by hope in view of God's mercy as he satisfied his wrath in his one and only Son, our willing substitute (Rom. 3:25–26).

There is a focused effort in our ministry—communicating words that carry our only assurance of hope, which is the gospel (Rom. 10:13–17). There is no creative ministry that can compare to the Spirit's ministry of creating a people for God by his Word. Our truthful words are arrayed in corresponding and beautiful adorning acts of love and compassion as we suffer in various ways to advance the gospel (Matt. 5:16; Gal. 6:10). These light and momentary sufferings range from giving our time when it is inconvenient to giving our lives when the world deems they are not yet spent.

So in view of God's mercy, we present our body as a living sacrifice, holy and acceptable to God, which is our spiritual worship (Rom. 12:1). This is no haphazard, reckless thing to do, because of the bulwark of certainty we are promised in that God has claimed for himself people from every tribe and nation, and these sheep will hear his voice (John 10:16; Acts 18:10; Rev. 5:9). And we do it all with joy for love—*for love*! Our sacrificial service only makes sense in light of God's future grace to us in Christ Jesus. Why else would we give like this if we didn't have a better and lasting possession (Heb. 10:34)? If we don't believe the promise that one day we will see his face and live (Rev. 22:4; see also Ex. 33:20; Matt. 5:8; 1 Cor. 13:12; 1 John 3:3), how can we face sacrificial service today?

Just like other healthy, growing believers in our congregation, we long to serve with the gifts God has given us. We must be focused and certain that as we reach out to others in love, it is with the proclamation of the crucified and risen Savior as the unapologetic heart of our message. The proclamation of the gospel while adorning its beauty by our lives has to be our chief aim in ministry, or we risk a deplorable inauthenticity.[18] Christians, by nature, are a people indwelt by an indomitable Spirit, and he longs to see the church built up and all God's children safely hidden in Christ.

Our Weaknesses Are Not in the Way

In our efforts to learn to love the bride of Christ, it is critical that we understand and grasp by faith that Christ's strength is made perfect in our weakness. We tend to assess our potential for serving in ministry by looking at our unique abilities, God-given talents, intellectual capacity, free time, and even our social-media influence. We look to these things partly because they are enjoyable, good things and partly because we can measure them. Discerning our giftedness and seeking out ways to profitably steward them are instrumental to our service to the body. But we are not to focus on the gifts themselves in our service; our focus is to be on Christ. When our focus is on the one who empowers us, enables us, and provides opportunities in which we may usefully serve him, we can even see the strategic way that God chooses to leverage our *weaknesses* to give him glory.

Consider how the difference between gifts and strengths flips our perspective on its head:

We tend to think of our strengths as inherently part of our identity. Strengths are our value-add; our competi-

tive edge. But gifts connote grace. A gift does not origi-
nate with us. It's something we receive from God and
steward for his sake. Therefore our gifts are not so much
our identity as our offering. And since God has given us
these gifts, he's not obliged to always put us in places
where we can use them fully. In fact, God frequently
places us in positions where we struggle and feel weak
for the very reason that he receives particular glory by
showing his strength *through* our weaknesses.[19]

Paul's thorn in the flesh, in 2 Corinthians 12:1–10, teaches
us that weakness isn't in the way—it is the way. For the sake
of God's glory we have an explicit, practical response to our
frailty and troubles: "For the sake of Christ, then, I am content with weaknesses, insults, hardships, persecutions, and
calamities," Paul says (v. 10). This is easier said than done,
of course, but we are not without help and hope in our endeavor to make much of Christ in our everyday lives. Look
at the very next sentence in verse 10: "For when I am weak,
then I am strong." It is not your power but Christ's power
working in you.

Consider Paul's famous prayer letter—Philippians. In
that letter he did not write (as I am so often tempted to write),
"Dear Friends, pray with us for [insert hardship here], because maybe God will use it. Lord willing. We sure hope so.
Cross your fingers for this one. Amen." Not at all. Paul wrote:
"I want you to know, brothers, that what has happened to me
has really served to advance the gospel" (Phil. 1:12).

Did he really say that the God who created everything from nothing was speaking his church into existence via a man in chains in a cell who preached the gospel? Yes, yes, he did. And the only reasonable explanation for this is astonishing, subversive grace. Friends, we are completely missing the point of Paul's jail time if we think it is remarkable how God used him *despite* his chains. We miss the point if we think that it is incredible that God uses any of us *despite* our weaknesses and frailty. God promises to strongly support us when we are weak, so there is no better place for us to be than right smack-dab in the middle of whatever weakness we are beset with, if we are in the middle of it in Christ. This is the kind of wisdom that leaves the rulers and authorities and the powers dumbfounded. "Great is the LORD, and greatly to be praised; *he is to be feared above all gods*" (Ps. 96:4). That's why Paul tells his Ephesian friends not to lose heart because of his suffering (Eph. 3:13).

If you're thinking what I'm thinking at this point, you're thinking that it is well and good to tell your friends not to lose heart, but it's another thing to be encouraged when the circumstances of your life feel like a pressure cooker. Weaknesses look bad, and, worse, they feel bad. Even as I assess my potential to be used by God according to human metrics-like influence, all the while knowing that's not the whole story, I don't personally want to be the first person to volunteer for discomfort or hard work. *What about me?* is my heart's nervous beat. Also, I prefer to look like I have everything together. Or, even better, I prefer to truly have everything together. It is exactly in this thinking that our minds need to be renewed by God's Word, because we so quickly forget that supernatural ministry carried along by grace involves more than meeting our human expectations and potential.

Christ promised us that his grace would be sufficient, and it always is—*always*. I'm sure you can point to your work in ministry and affirm that Jesus has always given you the grace you need. That is certainly true of our efforts in church planting here in the Arabian desert. We like to tell our supporters that we feel like reporters, just telling you the stories of what God is doing. Jesus deserves the credit and the glory for building his church in this place, and we get the joy. We are certainly accumulating real pain and even real scars along the way, but none of these things is worth comparing to the glory that will be revealed to us on a day that is coming very quickly (Rom. 8:18).

Grace flips my timid prayer letter on its head to read this way instead: "Friends, pray with us in this hardship because God will show himself to be faithful beyond the shadow of a doubt. And we want to be ready to praise him in all things together with you." Amen.

Weak Ministry

Our potential to minister to others is not measured by our gifts but by our God, who gives us everything we need to do everything he calls us to do. Therefore, we minister out of our weakness so that Christ's strength is on display. We are not able to minister to other people because we are the minister's wife, a seminary graduate, a mother, or a wife, or because we have a certain spiritual gift. The reason we can minister to others is that God himself has provided everything through his Son's work on our behalf and the Spirit's application of it to our lives. We have nothing eloquent or wise or caring to advise someone spiritually outside of God's Word. The fountain of living water is Christ himself, and he has purchased for us every spiritual blessing (Eph. 1:3).

Do you need help? Friendship in a lonely season? Boldness to kill sin? Discernment in choices? All these things are yours in Christ Jesus, and he amply supplies all that you need. God's Word leads us to pray as we see that he is the one who has wisdom, and he will give it generously to the one who asks (James 1:5).

One of the main ways we minister in weakness is through prayer. Prayer is an expression of our dependence on God for everything, telling us and him and everyone else that we are not adequate in and of ourselves. Keep a membership directory for your church nearby so you can remember to pray for your brothers and sisters.

Bless the elders and leaders of your church by praying for them regularly. Rather than being preoccupied with potential relational politics, pray. Rather than imagining issues that will influence your husband so that you grow anxious about them, pray. Rather than begrudge and bel-lyache about all the work your husband must do, pray that God would raise up more godly men to aspire to be elders and deacons and share the noble task (1 Tim. 3:1). Elders, like your own husband, are all sinners in need of a Savior. Pray that they will make the aim of all they do "love that is-sues from a pure heart and a good conscience and a sincere faith" (1 Tim. 1:5). Pray that the elders would persist in keep-ing a close watch over their lives and teaching (1 Tim. 4:16). Pray that as a band of brothers united in Christ, the elders together might love the appearing of the Lord Jesus, and look forward to that day when the righteous judge rewards them (2 Tim. 4:8). Pray that God would give them the grace they need to stay the course and reach the shore of heaven, not swerving from faithful doctrine, and avoid shipwreck-ing their faith (1 Tim. 1:6, 19). Pray that they would look forward to giving an account to Jesus for the flock they shepherd (Heb. 13:17). And, finally, thank the Lord for the gift of pastors and teachers. Jesus intentionally designed his church this way, giving the gift of godly leaders to shep-herd his people (Eph. 4:11).

One-Anothering in Weakness

However weak you may be or feel, the promised presence of God's indwelling Holy Spirit in you means that your con-tribution to fellowship is of profound value to others. This is the story we tell when we have been in the presence of a dear saint who is struggling in some way, and we walk away having been blessed by them when we thought we were going to be the ones doing the blessing. We dare not ever underappreciate the significance of the fact that *the Spirit of God* personally leads us to love our brothers and sisters. Do you lack guidance or direction in your service? Pray and ask the Lord to lead you and seek out his revealed will in his Word. We receive wisdom for breathless service unto the Lord by the very breath of God, which is his written Word. The scriptural *one anothers* give us a great place to start when we're stuck with gifts in our hands and not sure of how to share them. Here are just a few:

> A new commandment I give to you, that you love one another: just as I have loved you, you also are to love one another. (John 13:34)

> Love one another with brotherly affection. Outdo one another in showing honor. (Rom. 12:10)

> Therefore welcome one another as Christ has welcomed you, for the glory of God. (Rom. 15:7)

> Finally, brothers, rejoice. Aim for restoration, comfort one another, agree with one another, live in peace; and the God of love and peace will be with you. (2 Cor. 13:11)

> For you were called to freedom, brothers. Only do not use your freedom as an opportunity for the flesh, but through love serve one another. (Gal. 5:13)

> Bear one another's burdens, and so fulfill the law of Christ. (Gal. 6:2)

> But exhort one another every day, as long as it is called "today," that none of you may be hardened by the deceitfulness of sin. (Heb. 3:13).

God has designed our body-building service to be strategic in advancing his kingdom. Our love for one another says things about who Jesus is, and we can't witness to the unbelieving world of our loving unity unless there are others to whom we are united in brotherly love. In our efforts to serve one another in the body of Christ, we are reminded that we are *all* dependent on Christ, who is our head, for everything we need. As we are served the Lord's Supper, we are given a tangible way to taste that Christ's body and blood were "given for *you* [plural]" (Luke 22:19). To *him* be the glory in the church forever. Indwelled by God's Spirit, each of us (with our weaknesses and all) becomes the hands and feet of Christ himself to the praise of his glory in the universe.

God uses the weak things to shame the strong and to humble us so that "no human being might boast in the presence of God" (1 Cor. 1:29). When we think about the implications of how God works, we see that this is what we really want. We only *think* we want to get to the end of a long day of ministry and say, "I totally nailed it! Gimme a high-five, Jesus! Thanks for being such a great cheerleader."

Of course that's not what we really want. What we really want is to humbly depend on our loving Father who ordains all things, consciously give our burdens over to Jesus, and walk by faith as the Spirit leads us. We don't want to look to ourselves; we want to look to God's Word, where the Spirit of God has breathed out encouragement for us—promises to cling to as we seek to serve others.

In the face of criticism from people we thought were friends, in the middle of a 24-7 schedule of lots of work left undone, on the hard road of suffering or obscurity or misunderstandings or uncertainty in decisions, we want Christ's strength. We want to boast in our weaknesses so that Christ gets the glory for all our grace-driven efforts to love others (2 Cor. 12:9). We want to say with the apostle Paul, "By the grace of God I am what I am, and his grace toward me was not in vain. On the contrary, I worked harder than any of them, though it was not I, but the grace of God that is with me" (1 Cor. 15:10). We want to worship with the psalmist, "My flesh and my heart may fail, but God is the strength of my heart and my portion forever" (Ps. 73:26). We want to live as God's invincible servants under his loving care, commissioned to go out into the world and serve as his hands and feet for as many days as he has ordained in the strength that he supplies.

Conclusion

Here Comes the Bridegroom!

At the beginning of this book I asked, "What finite heart could hold all these things?" Indeed, our hearts cannot hold these things, but Jesus can, and he does, and he strengthens our hearts by his grace.

One of my favorite hymns is "The Sands of Time Are Sinking" by Anne Cousin. She penned this beautiful song over 150 years ago. Her pen scratched out this line that comes to my mind often: "The bride eyes not her garment, but her dear bridegroom's face." Isn't that just so true? When you are preparing for your wedding, it is so easy to get wrapped up in the details, especially that of your dress. We take great concern and care for our wedding dress, don't we? Every detail must be perfect. But the church is the only bride who doesn't have to worry about what she is going to wear. Our wedding garment has been provided for us by the groom himself; it has been granted us to be arrayed in the righteousness given to us by Jesus.

Anne's song is about prizing the presence of Christ himself, who is to be cherished over and above all his blessings. Indeed, we are each gifted for service as part of Christ's bride, the church. Yet we are not obsessed with Jesus's stuff but with Jesus himself. As we long for our heavenly bridegroom, we don't stand at the altar admiring the lace on our wedding dress; we watch the doors with great anticipation of Jesus's arrival.

The lives we live as we wait for Christ's return are to be marked by *distinctly Christian* love. In John 13:34 Jesus gave us a new command: "A new commandment I give to you, that you love one another: just as I have loved you, you also are to love one another." It's new because of what God had earlier commanded in Leviticus 19:18: "You shall not take vengeance or bear a grudge against the sons of your own people, but you shall love your neighbor as yourself: I am the LORD." How is this love for others distinctly Christian? Jesus zeroes in on what makes Christian ministry distinctly Christian—we love others *as he loves us*. In John 15:9–14 Jesus expands on what he means:

> As the Father has loved me, so have I loved you. Abide in my love. If you keep my commandments, you will abide in my love, just as I have kept my Father's commandments and abide in his love. These things I have spoken to you, that my joy may be in you, and that your joy may be full. This is my commandment, that you love one another as I have loved you. Greater love

has no one than this, that someone lay down his life for his friends. You are my friends if you do what I command you.

The apostle John reminds us of this too: "This is the message that you have heard from the beginning, that we should love one another" (1 John 3:11). And, again, he reminds us: "Now I ask you, dear lady—not as though I were writing you a new commandment, but the one we have had from the beginning—that we love one another" (2 John 5).

Only the strengthening grace of Jesus empowers us to love as Jesus loves. Ministry will ask so much from your husband, from you, and from your family. Circumstances, incidents, situations, and the people involved in them may ask for things you do not have and cannot give, which is to be expected. And the Lord of glory would have it no other way. There is no amount of God-honoring selflessness that you can muster apart from Jesus. The life that our loving heavenly Father has ordained for you will come along with divine appointments that expect much from you but never, ever, *ever* more than what God can supply. Sometimes God's supply comes in the form of learning to say (or clearly *needing* to say) no to opportunities. Other times he provides by sending workers into the harvest to share in the harvest with you. At the end of the day, the point isn't so much *how* God provides but the fact that *God* is the one who provides.

Ministry wives the world over, regardless of the expectations they live under or embody, can look forward with great anticipation to one expectation we are sure to meet. At the end of our days we will be astonished and overjoyed to see how our Chief Shepherd has unfailingly carried us through to this great feast of grace:

> After this I heard what seemed to be the loud voice of a great multitude in heaven, crying out,
>
>> "Hallelujah!
>> Salvation and glory and power belong to our God,
>>> for his judgments are true and just;
>> for he has judged the great prostitute
>>> who corrupted the earth with her immorality,
>> and has avenged on her the blood of his servants."
>
> Once more they cried out,
>
>> "Hallelujah!
>> The smoke from her goes up forever and ever."
>
> And the twenty-four elders and the four living creatures fell down and worshiped God who was seated on the throne, saying, "Amen. Hallelujah!" And from the throne came a voice saying,
>
>> "Praise our God,
>>> all you his servants,
>> you who fear him,
>>> small and great."

Then I heard what seemed to be the voice of a great multitude, like the roar of many waters and like the sound of mighty peals of thunder, crying out,

"Hallelujah!
For the Lord our God
    the Almighty reigns.
Let us rejoice and exult
    and give him the glory,
for the marriage of the Lamb has come,
    and his Bride has made herself ready;
it was granted her to clothe herself
    with fine linen, bright and pure"—

for the fine linen is the righteous deeds of the saints.

And the angel said to me, "Write this: Blessed are those who are invited to the marriage supper of the Lamb." And he said to me, "These are the true words of God." (Rev. 19:1–9)

We, the ones who are invited to this feast, are by grace turned into fellow inviters, along with all our brothers and sisters, until all the lost sheep are brought together under our one Chief Shepherd.

Notes

1. Dear reader, I am not so naïve as to think that every ministry wife reading this book is married to a man who fears the Lord and embraces Christlike servant leadership as his model in being a husband. I am very sensitive to the reality of domestic abuse, even in marriages in which people are serving in ministry. If you are living in a situation in which you are experiencing abuse of any kind (physical, sexual, verbal, spiritual, psychological, or emotional), I urge you to seek out help from trusted authorities, trusted church leaders, family members, or close friends in your life. Hopefully, you know trustworthy people who can support you. However, that may not be the case; in many situations only one or two such support structures are available. If you feel that your life or that of your children is in danger, please seek refuge somewhere safe. If you are experiencing abuse or supporting someone who is, please visit this website for more information and support on how to move forward: http://justinholcomb.com/making-a-safety-plan/.
2. John Piper, *Let the Nations Be Glad!: The Supremacy of God in Missions*, 3rd ed. (Grand Rapids, MI: Baker Academic, 2010).
3. I believe that the Bible is clear that God calls qualified men (as opposed to women) to serve as elders/pastors (1 Tim. 3:2; Titus 1:5-9).
4. Martyn Lloyd-Jones, *Fellowship with God: Studies in 1 John* (Wheaton, IL: Crossway, 1993), 62–63.
5. For an excellent, thorough discussion of identifying idols, please see Timothy Keller's *The Gospel in Life Study Guide: Grace Changes Everything* (Grand Rapids, MI: Zondervan, 2010).

6. I'm thankful to Paul David Tripp for pointing this out so clearly in his excellent book *What Did You Expect?: Redeeming the Realities of Marriage* (Wheaton, IL: Crossway, 2010).

7. Horatius Bonar, *The Everlasting Righteousness*, available in PDF from Monergism.com, http://grace-ebooks.com/library/Horatius%20Bonar /HB_Everlasting%20Righteousness,%20The.pdf.

8. Richard Sibbes, *Glorious Freedom: The Excellency of the Gospel above the Law* (Carlisle, PA: Banner of Truth, 2000), 69.

9. John Francis Wade, "Adeste Fideles," thirteenth century.

10. Sibbes, *Glorious Freedom*, 83.

11. William Still, *The Work of the Pastor*, rev. ed. (Ross-shire, UK: Christian Focus, 2010), 17.

12. John Piper, "Prayer: The Work of Missions," conference message (July 29, 1988), http://www.desiringgod.org/conference-messages/prayer -the-work-of-missions.

13. C. S. Lewis, *The Screwtape Letters* (New York: HarperCollins, 2009), 5. See also Song 6:4, where the king delights in his bride: "You are beautiful as Tirzah, my love, lovely as Jerusalem, awesome as an army with banners."

14. For further reading on this topic, may I commend G. K. Beale's worshipful and thought-provoking work *The Temple and the Church's Mission: A Biblical Theology of the Dwelling Place of God* (Downers Grove, IL: InterVarsity, 2004).

15. Mark Dever, *The Church: The Gospel Made Visible* (Nashville: B&H Academic, 2012), ix.

16. Beale, *The Temple and the Church's Mission*, 370.

17. Brian Croft and Cara Croft, *The Pastor's Family* (Grand Rapids, MI: Zondervan, 2013), 86.

18. "The mark of New Testament authenticity is first and foremost proclamation of the crucified and risen Jesus as the indispensable and irreplaceable heart of the Christian message." Carl F. H. Henry, *God, Revelation, and Authority* (Wheaton, IL: Crossway, 1999), 4:365.

19. Jon Bloom, "Don't Focus on Your Strengths," Desiring God blog (March 2, 2012), http://www.desiringgod.org/blog/posts/dont-focus-on-your -strengths.

General Index

Scripture Index

ALSO AVAILABLE FROM

Gloria Furman

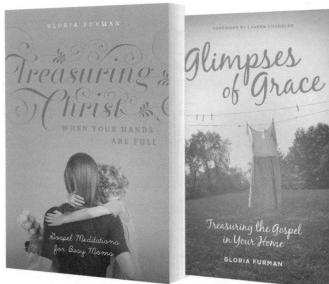
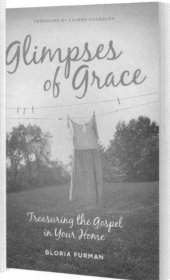

For more information, visit crossway.org.